THE NEXT 100 YEARS
*Predictions to the Nations
and the Church of the
21st Century*

THE NEXT 100 YEARS

*Predictions to the Nations
and the Church of the 21st Century*

DENNIS CRAMER

The Next 100 Years
Predictions to the Nations and the Church of the 21st Century

Dennis Cramer Ministries
328 Lowe Street
South Williamsport, PA. 17702
Phone: (570) 320-7757
Fax: (570) 320-0857
Email: denniscramer@suscom.net
Website: www.denniscramer.net

ISBN 1-886296-31-6
Printed in the U.S.A.
Original date of Part Two:
Predictions to the Nations, October 1997
Copyright 1998
First Printing 1998
Second Printing 2003

To order books contact:
Arrow Publications
P.O. Box 10102
Cedar Rapids, Ia. 52410
Phone: (319) 395-7833
Toll Free: (877) 363-6889 (U.S. only)
Fax: (319) 395-7353
Website: www.arrowbookstore.com

DEDICATION

To the nations of the earth who
will one day worship Jesus Christ.
"Who shall not fear You, O Lord,
And glorify Your name?
For You alone are holy.
For all nations shall come and
worship before You,
For your judgements
have been manifested."
(Rev.15:4)

CONTENTS

CONTENTS

INTRODUCTION

THE NEXT 100 YEARS!

The ministry of the prophet will have increased spiritual and secular significance in the 21st century.

Both the world and the Church — the unsaved and the saved — are voicing a deep desire to know the future. Already, this new millennium has become an obsession — even an unhealthy infatuation for some. Both sinner and saint have preoccupied themselves in a sort of end-times frenzy, seized by either an optimistic anticipation known as "faith" or a paralyzing mentality known as "fear."

Everybody wants to know what is going to happen, for good or bad, during this next millennium. Inquiring minds grasp for a sense of futuristic security in a search for meaning and purpose.

Are legitimate answers available? Can reasonable people expect to find direction and significance in the 21st century?

PREPARING FOR THE BRIDEGROOM

As Christians, we are living in the most exciting time in all of human history. According to the Bible, we are in the last days. In fact, we have been in the last days for 2000 years.

Jesus Christ will return to earth to receive His bride. Yet, it is equally true that He will not be hurried. Even Jesus Himself does not know the day or the hour of His own return. The Bible says only the Father knows this information — and no one else.

Our sincere yet feeble attempts to determine the exact time of His return are nothing more than pure speculation, sanctified guess work, and a dangerous private interpretation of the Bible. I consider it risky presumption at best.

This book is not about the Second Coming of Christ. I have absolutely no ideas when Jesus will return. I only know He will return, and that I am ready.

My focus is on His beautiful bride, the universal Christian Church. I am writing about how this bride, seen corporately through the nations of the world, is making herself ready for the Bridegroom's return.

EARTH-SHAKING AND CHURCH-CHANGING

In the early autumn of 1997, God surprised me and began to speak to me at length regarding the next 100 years. What I initially thought would be a typical sermon suddenly evolved into something much more.

He began to speak to me about the ever-increasing significance of the ministry of the prophet in the 21st century, providing me with details that developed into a kind of prophetic mandate from heaven. God gave me some insight into how the ministry of the prophet — a new breed of prophet — will impact not just the Church but the nations.

These 21st-century prophets are just some of the bridesmaids readying this beautiful, radiant, chaste bride for the wedding day. And what a wedding it will be!

This book is about the ever-increasing role of the New Testament prophets to the nations in the 21st century. These prophets will have a clear, biblical destiny to fulfill, and God will make sure these humble servants get the job done. It is part of His perfect eternal plan.

I have chosen to share with you what God has shared with me about these end times — however long they may last and for however long the Son of God may tarry.

The first part of this book presents the exciting transformation that will take place with the prophets of the 21st century. This almost overwhelming transformation will be earth-shaking and Church-changing for sure!

The individual price tag for this transformation will no doubt discourage some from moving on in God. Some will never know His best for their lives. Others — true disciples of Christ — will gladly pay the price as they envision the eternal crown, the reward that awaits them for their unselfish obedience.

In a word, these next 100 years will be about change — great change. It will be a time to put our hands to the plow and not look back.

WHAT IS GOD DOING?

Signs of the times abound, bringing with them many questions. Most Christians are asking: What is God doing?

Almighty God is wonderfully, powerfully, and sovereignly aligning the nations of the earth as it pleases Him!

Like giant pieces of a colossal global puzzle, the nations are being arranged with great precision in accordance with God's perfect, predetermined plan.

What will happen when this global puzzle is complete and all its pieces are secure in their proper place? The whole earth will be filled with God's glory in a clear fulfillment of Scripture! Be assured, the whole earth and all its nations will know and reverently fear the Lord of glory.

The second part of this book outlines a number of stirring prophecies God gave me for various continents, nations, regions, states, and even some cities.

Isaiah 40:15 refers to the nations as "drops in a bucket" and "small dust" and these lands of the world as a "very little thing." Still, God deeply loves nations. Why? Nations are full of people, and God passionately loves people.

God, however, is still God. He reigns supreme over all the earth and will not tolerate any attempt by any continent, nations, region, state, or city to usurp His preeminence. After all, the earth is the Lord's; it does not belong to nations. Nations belong to God. He owns them.

God is about to alter radically and permanently the face of the world and Church!

God knows precisely what He is doing. Omnipotent, omniscient, and omnipresent, God is in charge — not man, not the devil, not judges, rulers, princes or kings, not generals or armies, economists or politicians.

The God of heaven, the God of the Bible, the God of Abraham, Isaac, and Jacob rules and reigns supreme. He is in absolute control, and He is aligning the nations according to His perfect and eternal plan.

How will this global alignment be realized and who will help facilitate His predetermined plan? The prophets. These anointed representatives, this new breed of 21st century prophets, will collectively emerge in these same nations in unprecedented power and authority! They will be God's eyes, ears, and mouth!

"KISS THE SON"

The final aligning of the nations has begun, and God forgive any nation whose God is not the Lord. "Kiss the Son, lest He be angry, and you perish" (Ps. 2:12) will take on new significance in the 21st century. It will not be business as usual.

The time for nations to repent will suddenly present itself, and those same nations will be given only a brief window of opportunity to turn to God. To the same degree that God will continue to be a merciful God, He will reveal Himself to be a holy God, growing increasingly impatient with the sins of nations.

Truly, for some nations of the earth, it will be "fearful thing to fall into the hands of the living God."

Nations who choose to fear His name and serve Him will realize great national blessing. It will be their finest hour — the crowning glory for many nations.

Nations in rebellion to God during the next 100 years will experience a most difficult time — a period of severe judgment from a righteous and just God. Nations who have rebelled in times past will find mercy is still readily available for them, but the time to appropriate this mercy from God will grow short.

Whether a nation is ripped apart at its very foundation or openly blessed by God will depend on choices that nation makes before God. Some nations will die because of wrong choices, and others will live because of right choices. It's going to be that simple.

Righteous national choices will mean a nation will be strengthened and given longevity and honor among the other nations. Unrighteous national choices will mean the opposite — weakness, brevity, and shame on a national level. There will be no middle ground, no easy way out, no acceptable compromise with God. Nations will bow down before God one way or the other — voluntarily or involuntarily — but they will all bow!

Based on these choices, God will either show His loving kindness to a nation, or He will visit that nation with harsh judgments. A nation's own choices will determine whether its life span is extended or cut off prematurely, and it will have no one to blame but itself. Nations will reap precisely what they sow. It will be a time for the nations to choose life or choose death.

The 21st century will be about critical choices with national repercussions. The decision that a nation makes for or against the God of Abraham, Isaac, and Jacob will determine whether it is blessed or cursed.

Will a nation experience flies, frogs, lice, boils, locusts, and death? Or will a nation choose to embrace the Prince of Life and prosper in every conceivable way? This is the ultimate question facing all nations.

SOME FULFILLMENT

Already, in the first four years of this new millennium we have seen some of the events written about in this book coming to pass since first writing it in October of 1997. Indeed, the nations are being aligned by God!

In writing this book, I did no academic research of any kind, read no other books on the subject, and consulted with no one except the Holy Spirit. I had no personal, natural knowledge concerning any of the information about which I wrote.

By many standards, I am a rather simple person. I am not particularly politically minded and know little or nothing about economics, war, or weather. I simply have not had the time or much interest to keep up with current events. I don't subscribe to a newspaper or weekly magazine. I am not a historian or a futurist. I am a Christian who heard from God.

As a matter of fact, my personal opinion conflicted with a number of the revelations God gave me while writing this book. At times, I even wrote exactly opposite of what is currently happening on the earth.

Yes, I have stepped out of the boat, but faith is about taking risks — sometimes big ones! But God never asked me for my opinion, just my obedience. In fact, these revelations were a big surprise to me and came at an inopportune time when I was looking forward to a period of rest.

I did not solicit God for this information. God initiated the exchange, and I received it. He spoke, and I wrote it down.

I now present it to you again in it's original form. Not a word has been changed from the original prophecy given to me in October, 1997.

PART ONE

*Prophetic Power
and the Church*

ONE

Prophetic Power

The 21st century prophets will
display incredible spiritual power

L ed by a new breed of "power prophets," the 21st century will be the beginning of the "greater works" era for the universal Church of Jesus Christ. A sudden, almost instant worldwide release of these prophets will occur with signs and wonders following as God clothes them with an incredible, supernatural mantle of healing power.

SUPERNATURAL HEALING POWER

Signs, wonders, healing, and miracles on a large global scale will be visible to all — believer and unbeliever alike. Empty wheelchairs will pile up like mountains in hospitals, Churches, stadiums, and street corners. All manner of skin diseases will vanish before our eyes.

Incurable diseases like cerebral palsy and muscular dystrophy will be healed by the power of God. Deaf ears will open routinely. Blind eyes will see. Those who have lost the ability to speak will be healed and begin to sing the praises of God.

As the prophets travel far and wide to the nations of the earth, incredible healing miracles on a massive scale will take place. Twenty-four hour a day healing services will not be uncommon.

POWER EVANGELISM REVISITED

Then, suddenly, from out of this great prophetic, healing movement will come a new breed of power evangelists.

At first, these prophets and their counterparts, the evangelists, will look like twins, joined together as one, sharing vital organs, literally dependent on each other for their very existence. These men and women of God will not be easily distinguishable from one another.

Like anointed "Siamese" prophetic/evangelistic twins, they will work hand in hand with each other for a season until God sees fit to separate them. At the appointed time God will step in a begin a scheduled surgery, a procedure designed to save both twins and to increase their productivity ten-fold. Each ministry will take on a new and individual identity, each respecting the other.

The prophets will become God's pointers, giving direction to these Philip-like New Testament evangelists. The evangelists will become the pillars of this healing movement. It will be these 21st century evangelists who establish signs, wonders, healings, and miracles in the Church.

The 21st century prophets' role will be to "point" prophetically to certain geographical regions where healing will be poured out from heaven to the masses of people be-low. Then under prophetic mandate from these prophets of God, the 21st century evangelists will quickly respond by traveling to these pre-appointed places and realizing phenomenal results.

The prophets who were used of God to help initiate this great global healing explosion will not be responsible to finish it. That task will become the responsibility and the joy of these new power evangelists who will take divine healing to new heights and levels.

Together, the 21st century prophets and the 21st century

evangelists will see tens of thousands healed. Once again, the streets will be filled with those who walk, leap, and praise God!

"CUSTOM FIT" HEALING MIRACLES

Through the 21st century prophets, God will "custom fit" healing miracles to certain countries. Whole populations, major cities, and small towns alike will be freed from generations of specific sickness and disease that have plagued them for centuries!

Many out-of-the-way places — small, unknown, seemingly insignificant dots on the map-- will be powerfully blessed by God's provision of supernatural healing for chronic, incurable, deadly disorders. These small to medium size towns and villages will not necessarily be easily accessible by the masses, but this will not stop the flood of desperately ill people looking for physical relief and wholeness. God will not disappoint them.

For example, several coastal cities in the **Pacific Northwest** of the **United States** and some cities, towns, and villages slightly inland will see many mighty miracles of this kind — a real visitation from heaven!

Although some of these places will not even have airports, mile after mile of cars and buses will find their way there! A mighty healing revival will break out, gaining the attention of the unsaved population of this region. The Churches will not be able to handle the great influx of new converts — the result of this outpouring of undeniable, supernatural power.

Worldwide, all types of creative miracles will proliferate. Lost limbs will be restored, eyes will regenerate in their sockets, new teeth will miraculously fill people's mouths, bald heads will grow hair, missing bones will reappear, whole bodies will be covered with new skin, debilitating birth defects will vanish right before our eyes!

God will use these things to confound whole nations. Entire cities will shut down for days because so many of their residents are attending miracle meetings. Buses will run overtime, trains will overflow with eager passengers, highways will be filled with bumper to bumper traffic — all to transport people to these healing crusades.

Cities will erect monuments to commemorate where the glory of God fell, and there will be great joy as never before seen. It will be a joy that only Jesus Christ can provide. The world will never be the same!

Foul spirits will come out of many. Those who are possessed by them will scream and shout with a loud voice. People suffering from various palsies or who are crippled will be restored to health. Great crowds will heed what is spoken by these 21st century servants because of the miracles and wonders performed by them. The Church will once more experience the Book of Acts. We will witness it all again, and more, in the 21st century!

PROPHETS — EVANGELISTS — APOSTLES

Sometime after the 21st century evangelists are fully restored to their original New Testament status, another power impartation will take place — another changing of the guard. This next step in God's transformation of His Church will focus on His apostles.

Twenty-first century evangelists, having enjoyed several years of worldwide popularity, will impart their healing and miracle gifts to the apostles. But it won't stop there. An apostolic healing spree will take place!

As these powerful gifts and abilities are freely imparted to the New Testament apostles, something even more dynamic will occur. Signs and wonders will increase again in strength and in number.

Apostles will be vehicles of indescribable demonstrations of supernatural power, rivaling anything the prophets or evangelists did. Teams of apostolic workers will move like bands of Holy Spirit marauders, stirring up trouble for the devil wherever they go.

MASS CONVERSIONS FROM ISLAM

God will begin to specifically target His power toward certain people groups. One such group will be the **Muslim** populations of the earth.

Before God sends in any of His workers to preach the gospel of Jesus Christ, there will be unmistakable angelic visitations to thousands of Muslims worldwide. These divine interventions will set the stage for a sweeping evangelistic in gathering among the Muslim nations, especially Muslim nations in Africa and Asia.

These angels will break up the hardened soil of the hearts of Islam nations. As messengers of God's love and mercy, they will prepare the ground for the good seed of the gospel.

Contrary to many opinions about Islamic nations, the harvest will be easier and more abundant then many think possible. Due to the successful infiltration of the ranks of Islam by angels and by evangelists, many Islamic nations will see a significant decrease in actual numbers of Muslims within their borders. Mass conversions will stupefy any attempts at retaliation by fanatical followers of Islam. It will be a classic case of too little too late.

Unprecedented manifestations of healing will dazzle the Islamic world. God will show forth His awful might for all to see!

On the heels of this preparatory strike by these angelic messengers, God will send the second wave. These converted nationals from within their own countries will move swiftly, preaching and baptizing in the name Jesus.

An incredible underground Church will emerge and quickly establish itself as a rooted and grounded band of believers. Many Westerners will travel incognito, bringing their five-fold ministries with them to further equip and mature these new converts. Egypt will be prototypical of this new model of Muslim nation, which will turn to Christ in large numbers.

POWER TO LITTLE CHILDREN

The best news of all has to do with children of the 21st century. The greatest healings and miracles of all will be experienced by children.

There will be a worldwide release of healing over children through the prophets. It will quickly become apparent that God loves the little children as He performs miracle after miracle for these blessed ones.

Whole campaigns, entire evangelistic ministries, will change direction and begin to target children. There will be "children only" crusades all around the world.

God will show favor to many of these "little miracles" and will begin to use them in healing ministries themselves! The Church world and the secular world will be permanently changed through the healing hands of eleven and twelve-year-old children whose childlike faith will heal the sick, cast out demons, and raise the dead!

NATIONAL DELIVERANCES

The 21st century will witness the restoration of the "Moses" deliverance ministry. Once again God's divine presence will accompany the prophets much like it did for Moses.

Great supernatural power and authority will be granted these humble yet authoritative spokespersons. Through these mighty 21st century deliverers, whole geographical areas will experience release from ancient demonic atmospheres that had hovered over them for eons.

These prophets will begin to specialize in national deliverance just as Moses did. As a result, nations will experience the goodness of the living God.

Some of these deliverance prayers and prophecies will be televised for all to see. These new Moses-like prophets will once again cry out, "Let my people go!" God will deliver masses of people through the prophetic word spoken over their respective nations.

The Pharaoh-like spirit of control, manipulation, aggression, pride, and open defiance of God will not stand against His spoken judgments uttered by the prophets. Whole regions and entire nations will be liberated — permanently freed from the demonic culture to which they were once enslaved for centuries. The word of the Lord will accomplish this!

As with Moses in ancient times, the 21st century will see Jesus Christ hailed as the one true liberator! Nations will know "whom the son sets free will be free indeed."

Central America will experience some of the more powerful national deliverances from ancient curses, oaths, pledges, and covenants made by their ancient ancestors.

The spirit of human sacrifice lingers yet over this part of the world. The blood of innocent lives, which has cried out from the soil for centuries, will demand that national repentance for past sins be made. Although the actual practice has ceased, the insatiable hunger of this blood-thirsty, murderous spirit lingers, severely hindering this region of the world from experiencing the blessings of God.

To the Far East, portions of **Bangladesh, Nepal, Burma, India,** and **Bhutan** will be freed from the strongholds placed over them by their ancestors as well. Demonic forces will literally tear at the very fabric of these nations before they are driven away by the glorious light of the gospel of Jesus Christ.

Disasters on a cataclysmic scale, both natural and super- natural, will shake these countries to the core. The devil knows his days are numbered, and he will rip and tear, shout and scream on His way out. But be assured: He is on his way out! From the rising of the sun to the going down of the same, the Name of the Lord will be praised in **Bangladesh, Nepal, Burma, India,** and **Bhutan!**

Demonic devices, such as killer earthquakes and even more violent killer volcanoes, will cause confusion, fear, and national panic in this region. Yet, God will not abandon His people. Eventually, before all-out anarchy prevails, new civil governments will be born with righteous roots, and these troubled nations will know the loving favor of God.

God will raise up Ezekiel-like prophets for this part of the world, and they will prophesy to the nations. The "valley of dry bones" scenario will once again depict the power of the prophets to the nations.

These nations will be restored as the word of the Lord is spoken over them, and they will know prosperity and stability as they evolve into essentially Christian nations. Many prophets will go to the high places in these nations and prophesy over the cities below, speaking blessing over the masses of people.

Even the average life expectancy of people will dramatically increase almost overnight due to the repentance that takes place in their nation. God will grant long life to those who serve Him.

Sadly, some judgments will also be proclaimed against these people who refuse the God of Abraham, Isaac, and Jacob. Those bastard nations will continue to linger in abject poverty, perversion, and pestilence as darkness increases over them.

POWER OVER HINDUISM

During the 21st century the love of God will fall upon the Hindu peoples of the world. Because He loves the Hindu people, God will break the back of Hinduism, especially in India.

God says, "The yoke in India will be destroyed because of the anointing."

Hundreds of thousands of converts will stream into the kingdom of God from India alone. The Ganges River will be the biggest baptismal tank in the world!

As a great sweeping move of God begins in the south of India and rumbles northward like a mighty, rushing wind, India will feel the breath of God blow on her. Jesus Christ will be seen as the one true light of the eastern world.

More than one national crisis will arise, attempting to distract India from realizing her destiny among the nations. Political upheaval, warring neighbors, meteorological disasters, and more will occur. But the God of heaven is making a promise to the people of India:

"Oh ancient India your land will be a refuge for My people, a new land of Goshen for the oppressed, a new promised land, a new Beulah land. India will be My land," says the Lord, "a land flowing with milk and honey for the peoples of the world."

"My hand shall melt and mold you until you are molded and

shaped as I please," says the Lord.

"You were Mine in the beginning, and you will Be Mine again. Return to me, and I will return to you. Seek Me, and you shall live."

"Make no unholy alliances with heathen nations, neither pledge your power and might to the highest bidder. Fear the Lord and live. Bow to the wishes of man, and you will forfeit your place in the kingdom of God. Honor Me, and I will honor you."

JAPAN AND RUSSIA'S HOLY ALLIANCE

Japan will see unprecedented numbers of enthusiastic converts come to Christ. Her material wealth will be used for the glory of God.

Out from these new converts will come an army of Japanese prophets who will not be denied their opportunities from God. One of their first opportunities will lie just to the west of **Japan** along the coast of **Asia**.

Russian believers will gladly receive wave after wave of Japanese prophets, and **Russia** will not be able to stop the tide of "charismatic" Christianity from sweeping over her Churches from the east. No government decree by the Russians will be able to successfully halt this marvelous move of God.

There will be a new, holy alliance between Japanese and Russian Christians, another Jonathan and David covenant relationship. All ethnic, cultural, societal, and religious differences will be set aside for the greater purposes of Almighty God. Russian and Japanese Christians will wash one another's feet in humanity, following the example of their Lord.

A RUSSIAN REGIONAL REVIVAL

On the strength of this wonderful, working relationship between Japanese and Russian believers, a great revival will break out along the east coast of **Russia**. The revival will run along the shoreline from the Sea of **Japan** to the Sea of Okhotsk to the Bering Sea with the strongest concentration of revival fire located along the Russian shore of the Sea of **Japan**.

The Japanese Church will send all forms of aid, both material and spiritual, to their Russian brothers and sisters. This coastal region of **Eastern Russia** will be filled with smiling Russian believers greeting their smiling Japanese brothers and sisters. Joy and unity will be the trademarks of this move of the Spirit.

Airlines will have to schedule new flights, and shipping lines will have to begin new routes to accommodate the influx of people and resources into this area. Boom towns will spring up overnight, churches will be built, souls will be saved.

Material prosperity will come to this barren region of **Russia** as substantial new oil and mineral deposits are discovered. This boom will serve to bring people from all over the world to work there, and God will take full advantage of the opportunity as these workers are evangelized and sent back to their respective countries.

THE LAND OF THE RISING SON

God is already speaking to Japanese believers and instructing them to get ready for this great revival now. The Christian Church in Japan must begin to set aside their resources now. Be prepared for this event — it will happen suddenly.

This twenty-year long Russian revival will have a profound affect on **Japan** and literally reverse the nation's role in the global community of nations. As a result of this revival, the nation of **Japan** will become a generous country, revising its foreign policy to accommodate its new mission of caring for the less fortunate of the world.

Japan will continue to reach out to other less fortunate nations, bringing Christianity to many lands. Japanese Christians will radically affect many nations with their generous support and all-out commitment to evangelize the lost.

Japanese evangelistic ministries will travel worldwide, spreading the joy of the Lord and the need for personal discipleship in the Churches. Televised crusades broadcast throughout **Japan** will demonstrate to the Japanese people that God is a miracle-working

God. TV evangelism will skyrocket during the first ten years of the 21st century in **Japan.**

MOVING MASSES

There will be a repeat of the original exodus story in the Bible as nations are delivered from centuries of demonic oppression. Whole populations will shift from one location to another, critically affecting their countries' population bases.

These massive movements of people will be unstoppable by their respective governments. National borders will experience great change with the ebb and flow of populations, challenging the map makers of the world. The Spirit of God will sovereignly deploy His angels to lead masses of people over existing borders into new promise lands.

Because of these divine interventions, national bankruptcies will occur overnight, tax bases will crumble, civil unrest will run rampant. All manner of confusion will tear at any nation who does not take a stand for righteousness. Nations will reap exactly what they sow. God will not be mocked!

God will personally open the door to northern **Africa,** and Christianity will flourish. The borders of the countries which occupy northern **Africa** will change just as sand shifts when the winds blow over it. God will sovereignly blow over these nations, and their people will be renewed and refreshed under the wind of the Holy Spirit as a result of this marvelous and unexpected visitation of God!

All of this activity, this aligning of nations, will sometimes seem violent in nature, and will cause great concern for many in the universal Church. The Church, however, must remain focused on what God is doing on the earth and maintain a global vision.

We must see things as God sees things. We must remain committed to the Great Commission. We must not become alarmed at the unsettledness of nations. It is only the fulfillment of His plan for the earth. He is a sovereign God, and He said He would align the nations as it pleased Him and Him alone! Don't worry, God knows what He is doing.

PROPHETIC POLITICAL POWER

Having matured in their prophetic gifting through years of faithful obedience of God, prophets will begin to operate on new levels of prophetic authority. Worldwide, prophets will speak before civil governments, delivering powerful prophetic speeches to nations, literally shaking their existing political foundations.

Prophets who previously delivered one-on-one personal prophecy will begin to deliver powerful corporate prophecy to local Churches. Other prophets will proclaim accurate regional prophecy over large geographical regions, affecting tens of thousands of people in the process.

Finally, some of these prophets will begin to issue national prophecies — clear prophetic mandates from God on a national level. These powerful national prophecies, although harsh in nature at times, will provide entire nations with hope, destiny, purpose, and a future.

In some cases, these national prophecies will represent a nation's last opportunity for repentance. Consequently, new laws will be passed quickly in response to these life changing national prophecies as entire nations humble themselves and accommodate the "word of the Lord."

Sadly, other nations will reject the prophetic word spoken over them. For these stubborn nations, increased prophetic judgments will result.

Corrupt political systems will become a necessary target of these worldwide prophets. Consequently, these same prophets will have many political enemies as they zero in on evil men and their evil regimes. Governments will tremble!

GOD'S DYNAMIC DUO

The outcomes of many national elections will hang on the

intercessions of the saints, and these prayer warriors will begin to work closely with the prophets.

God will place many godly leaders in positions of political authority because of the powerful marriage between intercessors and prophets. The intercessors and prophets will be God's dynamic duo for the 21st century.

The prophets will give direction to the intercessors, and they in turn will birth many things for the kingdom of God.

The prophet will have much greater visibility than the intercessors, but these 21st century prayer warriors will be God's own secret weapons. Their powerful prayers will wreak havoc on the devil and His plans.

Prophets will feverishly solicit their prayer support, placing great value on the umbrella of protection these intercessors will provide them. To the 21st century prophet, these anointed, called, and legitimate intercessors will be more valuable than gold!

Some prophetic ministries will establish international networks of intercessors who will wage war in the heavenlies, tear down principalities, and destroy strongholds over nations. Prayer will become a lethal weapon in the hands of these skilled soldiers, and they will wield their weapons with deadly accuracy — taking no prisoners!

GOD'S POWER FOR BOTH SEXES

The 21st century will see both men and women occupy positions of intercession to the nations. This integration of the intercessors will be further proof that both sexes will do God's bidding with joy and effectiveness.

Both men and women will unite in God's power to the nations. Teams consisting of dynamic men and women — capable, able, empowered ministers of God — will flood into nations.

Men and women will intercede together before the Lord. Men and women will dance together before the Lord who made them. Men and women will occupy positions of great authority in the

Church. Men and women will fulfill their individual destinies. Rather than "compete," men and women will "complete" the work of Christ on the earth, displaying a new unity never before seen in the Church.

A new redemptive harmony will prevail. Just as overcoming racism was a major theme in the 90s, eliminating sexism will become a major theme in the 21st century. With its demise inevitable, its head will be cut off for all to see!

SUPERNATURAL METEOROLOGICAL POWER

All types of meteorological phenomenon will accompany these prophetic men and women of the God. The supernatural events will serve to dramatically accentuate the ministry of these 21st century prophets.

Their prayers will once again affect the heavens and the earth. Monsoons will ceases during their season. Crop fields will rise or fall depending on how the prophets are received. Snow will fall depending on how the prophets are received. Snow will fall where it has never snowed before — even unprecedented heavy snowfall in the summer!

God prophets will disrupt weather patterns both through their prophecies and through their presence. Yes, and their physical presence will cause marked meteorological changes to occur, causing blessing or cursing to settle over whole regions.

Which way the events of the day transpire will sometimes revolve around God's prophets. When prophets are blessed, God will bless. When prophets are harmed, God's wrath will arise.

BLOOD, FIRE, VAPOR OF SMOKE

Just as it was during the ministry of Jesus, the elements will submit to the command of the prophets! God will dramatically fulfill the last part of Joel's prophecy in Acts 2:19 for all the world to see. God said there would be "blood, fire, and vapor of smoke."

Blood, fire, and vapor of smoke speak of the full spectrum of meteorological signs and wonders that God will pour out upon the prophets in the last days,

God said emphatically, "I will show wonders in the Sky, and I will show signs on the earth." When God says, " I will," He means He will! Wonders will be seen from the heavens above, and signs will come from the earth below. God will do it through His prophets. All this and more will be witnessed by the Church and the world as the prophets demonstrate meteorological mastery.

For example, the waters of the **Mediterranean Sea** will be affected by a terrible plague — many living things in this body of water will die. Consequently, due to the death in the water that surrounds her, **Italy** will experience a national water shortage. This will be a sign of judgment from God.

God will also use the prophets to lift or terminate similar plagues from certain regions as well. As much as God will use the prophets to bring judgment, He will also use them to show great mercy to mankind.

Prophets will demonstrate both the loving kindness and the severity of God to the nations. Prophets will be invited to nations specifically to pronounce blessing over them. Even the value of certain currencies will escalate overnight to new heights because the prophets spoke blessing on that nation's economy.

INCREASED ANGELIC POWER

The overall activity of angels will drastically increase in the ministry of the 21st century prophet. God will assign warring angels to many prophetic ministries, and their exploits will be commonly known.

Prophets of all calibers will see consistent angelic intervention. The young, the old, the seasoned, the novice, the local prophets, the nationally assigned prophets will all find God's favor in beings assisted by His angels. These supernatural beings will do many mighty works as they accompany the 21st century prophets, becoming literal partners.

The nation of **Mexico** will witness many such angelic interventions as prophets scour this land, establishing Churches from shore to shore.

Some of the prophets will be transported in the Spirit from one geographical place to another, accompanied by their angelic partners. As these prophets are threatened with physical violence and death, their angels will come to the rescue, literally snatching the prophets of God from the jaws of death.

Angels will play an important part in the aligning of the nations. They will put their shoulders to many obstinate nations, shaking the very foundations upon which they stand. Political, economic, military, agriculture, and financial instability will sometimes be the result of this angelic shaking — and no amount of human intervention will make a difference.

God, not man, will have the last word!

TWO

PROPHETIC AUTHORITY

*The 21st century prophets will exercise
unprecedented authority*

An immeasurable, yet recognizable, spiritual authority made Jesus stand out in a crowd. In fact, this authority made Him the greatest prophet who ever lived — the prototype for all others to follow.

Jesus oozed authority. This authority came from pure obedience to the Father. With perfect surrender, Jesus never acted independent of the Father's heart. Dependence of God flowed forth from His life, not just the words. Jesus operated under the canopy of a totally surrendered will, devoid of any person human agenda.

Signs and wonders certainly helped Jesus to make His point, but it was authority that made Jesus so irrefutable. He never depended on outward manifestations of power to validate His authority, only to echo it. These phenomena only served to point the way to the Father.

Personally, Jesus had nothing to prove. There was no striving in Him, no need for self-promotion, no sense of self-importance. He knew who He was and where He was going. His mission and His purpose were clear. The authority that Jesus possessed superseded even the awesome miracles He performed.

Jesus had unmistakable, unlimited spiritual authority. This was evidenced in everything He said and did. It was the platform upon which He ministered as the Son of God. It was the license through which He successfully represented the kingdom of God. It was the secret to His power.

When Jesus spoke, the people could hear authority in His words. When He cast out devils, His hearers could feel authority in the atmosphere.

OOZING AUTHORITY

The same will be true for the 21st century prophets. The platform upon which they exercise their prophetic gifts, the license they wield to do greater works than Jesus, and the unstoppable secret to their power will be their authority that will rock the nations and change the face of the Church forever!

The 21st century prophets will be like Jesus — true anointed ones! They, too, will know who they are and where they are going in God. They will have nothing to prove, no man to please, no agenda to promote.

They will have no desire to be seen or heard outside of their appointed sphere of ministry. They will be God's secret weapons, and God's power will confirm them.

The anointing of Jesus Christ will rest heavily on them, and they will successfully co-labor with Christ. They will be an extension of His love and power to the nations.

This anointed company, consisting of men and women from every nation, will form a truly diverse group of young and old, rich and poor, male and female, adult and child — a prophetic enlistment on a grand global scale.

They will operate under the same canopy of perfect surrender, ooze the same spiritual authority, command the same respect, flow in the same river of manifestations, possess no personal agendas, and live lives worthy of their calling — just like Jesus!

PROPHETIC POWER DEFINED

What is authority, and why is it different from power? Many people confuse these two terms, thinking they are synonymous when, in actually, they are very different.

The 21st century prophets will experience a merging of power and authority — a marriage of these two dynamics into a perfect union. Yet, like a bride and bridegroom, there are wonderful differences — some obvious, others not so obvious.

So what is the difference between prophetic power and prophetic authority!

Power is defined as the natural existence of force. Nature provides a good example of this understanding of power in the field of solar energy.

Solar energy or solar power is simply the existent force of the sun. It is what the energy of the sun gives off naturally — what it releases, what it emits. In its natural state, solar energy is a pure, raw, unspoiled power, something intrinsic and inherent to the sun. It is a power that defines what the sun is because both define the other.

It will be the same with 21st century prophets. All will have a measure of power. This intrinsic power, this inherent dynamic, will come with the territory; it will simply be a part of the prophetic office. Like the example of the sun, prophets will possess existent force — supernatural power — simply because that is a part of what will make a person a 21st century prophet.

AUTHORITY: RIFLING GOD'S POWER

Power alone, however, will not fully define the prophet's role. A greater dynamic than mere power will emerge, eventually over-shadowing even their signs, wonders, healings, and miracles. The new identifying characteristic of the prophets will be an unmistakable prophetic authority.

By definition, authority is quite different from power. Authority is the acquired ability to use this pure raw power; to tap into this generous available dynamic; to harness it properly and completely; to channel it effectively; to successfully benefit from this force.

Authority harnesses power and utilizes it to its optimum, giving it meaning, purpose, and direction. Authority rifles power, focusing it, making it hit the mark. This is what will make true 21st century prophets different.

Authority is simply the effective use of all the particular skills one may posses. It is a combination of wisdom, knowledge, and experience. Authority gives anything it touches a permanency, making it last — making it productive and efficient.

This is precisely what the 21st century prophet's new authority will do for them. It will radically improve their ministry, making them ever more valuable, productive, and efficient. Authority — this is, the ability to rifle God's power — will define true biblical prophetic ministry in the 21st century, helping prophets to establish the Church of Jesus Christ.

Authority is what will make these 21st century prophets unchallenged experts in their field of ministry. These prophetic specialists, clothed with a new ability to dominate their respective field of ministry, will redefine prophetic gifting. They will rewrite the book on prophetic ministry because they will fully embrace both restored power and, more importantly, restored authority.

They will understand the meaning of the wedding between power and authority — this union of two supernatural dynamics, the joining of two truths — and will shake nations in the process.

IN-YOUR-FACE PROPHETS

Unprecedented prophetic authority will be the predominant trademark of the 21st century prophets — an authority the Church and the world has never before seen! It will be an authority that all of creation has long for — even groaned for — since time began.

Finally, these servants of God will manifest and come into their own. The 21st century prophets will take on a new appearance, a new demeanor, a new prophetic personality. They will be a company of dead-serious, no-holds-barred, get-in-your-face, time-to-play-hardball prophets. They will exude the kind of authority that will not win friends, but it will be a necessary authority — and it will be from God.

Signs, wonders, miracles, and healings — a wonderful God-ordained "show of force" to be sure — will only serve to gain the attention of the Church and the world. These displays of supernatural power will merely point to something greater, more permanent, something overdue — a much needed transformation.

This power exhibited by the prophets will be an incontestable prelude to an even greater release of true prophetic authority — a new, razor-sharp authority. A new prophetic authority — based on an acquired skill and mastery of their calling from God — will cut deep into the very soul of the Church, and the prophets will use surgeon-like skills to establish the Church for her greatest hour.

Although great encouragers to the Body of Christ, the prophets will begin to exercise this new level of authority by delivering divine rebukes, ultimatums, and judgments to individuals and nations in order to warn, correct, and discipline. As a result of this new authority, the prophets will be taken seriously because God Himself will see to it!

Ultimately, even signs and wonders will pale in the light of this new authority, taking a back seat to the exercise of the prophet's original purpose, which was and is to equip the Church for service.

AUTHORITY WILL RELEASE POWER

Increased prophetic authority will be the vehicle through which increased prophetic power is released — new authority will release new power!

This power will grow exponentially — both feeding off the other. This new authority of the prophets, an authority from heaven itself, will make them truly foundational ministers possessing legitimate government skills in the worldwide Christian Church.

Clad in this new armor of authority, the prophets will arise as one, an army capable of doing much harm to the kingdom of darkness. They will be God's dread champions, His frontline troops, His first wave, assaulting any and all enemies with a prophetic ferociousness.

Yet, the secret to their newfound authority will be a new level of surrender. A new surrender will breed a new and indomitable prophetic authority.

ELIJAH/ELISHA AUTHORITY

From out of the ranks of the 21st century prophets will arise yet another select group. These will be larger-than-life figures — men and women of God possessing even greater authority from God than other prophets.

The new millennium will see a return to and the restoration of the Old Testament prophetic model of Elijah and Elisha — prophets of fire like Elijah, and double-portion prophets like Elisha. Both will operate in an unabashed authority and will impact not just the Church — but literally all of mankind — as God backs their words. Not concerned so much with matters of the Church, these prophets will deal with non-religious issues among the nations. Once again, the fear and dread of the Lord will come on whole populations at the announcement that these "secular" prophets are coming!

Operating in untold power, they will announce prolonged droughts, depose rulers, miraculously feed the hungry, raise the dead, and destroy the false prophets of the world — and nations will tremble! In some instances these Elijah/Elisha prophets will bring disruption and chaos to nations as they openly and publicly confront the sin of these nations.

These seasoned prophetic veterans will be no-nonsense prophets, calling whole nations to decide whom they will serve, God or Baal, and openly challenging the powers of darkness in the process — just as Elijah and Elisha did.

Through prophecy, they will pray over nations with great authority, be accompanied by mighty angels, appoint and anoint kings (modern day leaders) — actually prophesying who will rule over a certain country and even predicting the results of national elections.

MARTYRS FOR THE KINGDOM

These politically-minded prophets will pronounce tremendous blessing on some nations and awful doom on others. They will be both loved and hated as a radical, fanatical minority, but the prophets will be clearly and unaplogetically sold out for God.

Some will have to flee for their lives as hostile, evil governments try to capture and kill them — a common historical reaction to God's prophets. They will not be silenced, however.

The Elijahs and Elishas are coming — those having twice the prophetic anointing, twice the prophetic mantle, twice the prophetic authority.

As oracles of God, they will be prophets of great extended vision, looking well into the future and giving many leaders — both in the Church and in the secular world — clear, accurate, prophetic direction.

Entire geographical regions will experience sudden overpowering fright, a sort of corporate panic, knowing that these Elijah/Elisha prophets have crossed the borders into their land.

Clandestinely, they will move in stealth-like prowess, infiltrating country after country with the glorious news of the gospel of Jesus Christ with unstoppable signs and wonders.

These new prophetic champions of the Lord will become both national heroes and heroines — as well as martyrs for the kingdom. The general populations of certain countries will enthusiastically receive these prophets, but just as vehemently their respective governments will purpose to kill them.

Even in death some of these Elijah/Elisha prophets will have a wonderful posthumous influence as the news of their deaths causes even greater revival fires to ignite!

Even in the face of martyrdom, these rare and priceless prophetic pioneers will proliferate. They will be the fearless reformers of the Church and the world in the 21st century.

Specifically, the Christian Church in China will seem to specialize in replicating many such Elijah/Elisha prophets.

THE RICH AND THE FAMOUS

The rich and the famous from around the world will also know the power and authority of the prophetic word.

Some prominent people outside the Church will receive prophetic direction and will confirm the accuracy of the prophetic word spoken over their lives — amazed at the prophetic nature of the revelations God had spoken through the prophets. They will admit the secrets of their hearts were revealed and will worship God, reporting to the world that the prophets of God are real!

Many 21st century prophets will experience as much prophetic success outside the four walls of the Church as they once had inside those same four walls.

Do not misunderstand the wisdom of God. His bride, the Church of Jesus Christ, will never be neglected; she will never be abandoned by the Bridegroom. The ministry of the prophet will simply expand to include both sinner and saint with both groups feeling the full effect of their authoritative prophecies, biblical teachings, and incontestable miracles.

Formal audiences with civil governments and, specifically, their legislative bodies will be a new focus of the 21st century prophets. They will speak to high-ranking secular leaders of all types, not only governmental but military leaders, financial tycoons, and politicians.

"Hollywood types" — those in the entertainment field and famous media personalities — will be confronted by the prophets as well! God will even grant an audience with at least one American billionaire, and He will repent, accepting Jesus Christ as Lord and savior.

These prophets will speak of future events in the lives of these individuals, causing some to repent. Others will laugh off the warnings of God, choosing instead to trust in riches and fame, and will die in their sins.

INTERNATIONAL "SUPER PROPHETS"

Epitomizing this new level of prophetic authority, three internationally recognized prophets from three different countries will emerge, having global influence and recognition. Virtually governing their respective countries and surrounding regions, they will walk in an unmistakable anointing.

These three individuals will be the high-ranking prophetic commanders of a huge international endtime prophetic army. They will be a spiritually-balanced yet spiritually bold trio — a human trinity of prophetic maturity and stability. This threesome will be a formidable foe to the kingdom of hell.

Heaven will openly endorse them, and hell will decry them. Fortunately, for the universal Christian Church, hell will not succeed in censuring these men of God. Their prophetic message will go out to the four corners of the earth. God will heard!

David: The "Love" Prophet

The first of these three internationally recognized individuals will be known as the "David" prophet. He will be a mighty warrior with actual military experience, a worshiping prophet with genuine musical talent, and a liberating king – a hero to many.

By worldly standards he will be seen as a renaissance man – A person of some wealth and culture. He will have the hightest profile of the three internationally recognized prophets, becoming a household name around the world.

Many will look to him during times of darkness and despair. His prophetic mantle will guide the Church through difficult seasons of persecution and martyrdom worldwide. He will exercise the most authority, being recognized as the senior of the three.

This English speaking prophet, a citizen of a democratic nation, will be known by some as the "love" prophet because of his emphasis on relationship and accountability. A prolific author, his prophetic writings will be greatly prized in many countries.

Above all, like the original David, this national leader will be a man after God's own heart.

Daniel: The Great Peacemaker

The second of these three "super prophets" will be known as the Daniel prophet.

Like the original Daniel, he will be a moral statesman: tactful, diplomatic, ambassadorial, yet uncompromising in his convictions as a Christian. Fearless, he will never hesitate to lay his life on the line.

As a wise discerner, this Daniel prophet will know the times and seasons of God, having his finger on the very pulse of what God will be doing on the earth. He will prophecy several major prophetic events and gain the attention of the nations.

This larger-than-life figure from a prominent family will have a history of unjust persecution having experienced political captivity as a young boy. He will be a highly educated man with at least one college degree and will marry late in life.

Several attempts will be made on his life. God, however will protect and promote him.

Pressures from other nations — ethnic, cultural, and even racial pressure -- will come down hard on this righteous, humble servant. Both Jew and Arab will vie for his loyalty. He will be coerced to sell out to those leaders who have less than godly motives but will not succumb to their tempting.

Like Daniel of old, this new Daniel will stand his ground against all odds and will emerge from his "fiery furnace" unscathed, uncompromised, and unharmed. Almost overnight, because he endured such hardship. God will advance him to a position of great authority over nations and regions.

Known as "the wisdom prophet" he will know strategies, have visions, and interpret dreams. He will be a classic seer, one who possesses telescopic spiritual vision — a real long-range planner.

Yet, the new Daniel will also be a highly practical man. He will be responsible for showing mercy and kindness to poorer nations. He will be a benevolent man, full of good works, generous even to his enemies, feeding and clothing them.

A **Middle Eastern** prophet of Jewish descent, this man will be far less traveled than His peers. He will stay at home but will prophesy to neighboring countries with great accuracy.

He will host conferences for other national leaders. These conferences will secure peace for nations previously at war with one another. He will be known as a man of peace among nations, earning the name, the "Great Peacemaker." The newspapers will frequently use this title to describe him and his successful efforts at making and maintaining peace. Some of his peace agreements will last indefinitely.

This man of God will be a watchman over Israel and especially **Jerusalem.**

The Joseph Prophet: A Leader of Leaders

Finally, there will emerge the Joseph prophet. He will be an interpreter of dreams and visions, a true man of the Spirit, as well as an expert economist and businessman.

This new Joseph prophet will show similarities yet apparent differences to the original Joseph of the Bible. This 21st century Joseph will not have the same history as the first Joseph.

He will be a man whose younger years were spent living a rather normal, even mundane life. Outwardly, he would not be the man most of us would have picked for the job. Unimpressive in appearance, this second Joseph will be the antithesis of the first in background and history.

Why then compare him to the Joseph of Genesis fame? It will not be a similar past that links him to the first Joseph but a striking similarity in his release into public service.

Almost overnight this man will be catapulted to global political fame. Like Joseph of Egypt, this new face will be a leader of leaders, a great motivator, a genius of organization, able to mobilize whole nations to accomplish great tasks for God. He will be a man of great resource, pooling together the nations in several economic accords that will further God's plan for the earth.

Although shy and unassuming, this Joseph, serving as God's catalyst, will bring the other two prophets together at pertinent times to coordinate strategies. Nations will eagerly await the prophetic directives coming forth from these prophetic summits.

INTERNATIONAL PROPHETIC TEAMS

Just as these three prophets join forces to be a part of something greater than themselves, other 21st century prophets all over the world will do the same.

Prophetic teams will begin to overshadow individual prophetic performances. There will be few prophetic stars, few church celebrities, even fewer prophetic performers. Instead, national and international prophetic affiliations, new associations, new organized bodies of worldwide prophets will be birthed.

These nameless and faceless prophets will embrace a new humility and see their authority in the prophetic explode, expanding far beyond anything they could have produced on their own.

Networks of international prophetic ministries will be common and multinational leadership will be the norm. This will not be an American-led crowd or a western-led crowd.

All nationalities will participate in this worldwide prophetic merging of various streams — a multinational, multi-ethnic, multi-racial confluence of prophets — a mighty prophetic river that will flood the nations.

PROPHETS RETURNING TO THE GATES

In ancient times, many cities were defended by massive physical walls and strategically placed gates. Essentially defensive structures, these fortifications were necessary to defend against hostile intruders. By their very construction, however, the gates of a city were the weakest point in its defenses and vulnerable to any attacking force.

The military minds of the day understood that to "possess the gates" of a city meant it had been taken in battle, enabling the invading army to control the inhabitants. The enemy thus occupied the city. Whoever controlled the gates controlled the city.

At the gates of a city, legal business was carried out, bargaining took place and important news was passed along. The gates were a place of brisk activity where commerce of all kinds was transacted daily.

Most importantly, the gates of a city were where the elders — the city fathers — "held court" or acted as overseers. They literally controlled what and who came into a city. In essence, these elders — created and controlled the overall environment of their city — either for good or evil.

In the 21st century, there will be a very important spiritual application for both gates and elders. Figuratively, "gates" reference the overall material and spiritual status of a city. "Elders" reference those whom God has positioned there to govern.

God will begin to bless cities because the perfect elders — the appointed prophets to that particular city — took their rightful place at the gates! Whole cities, entire populations will experience increased commercial influence. Local economies will soar, and material prosperity will shower down — all because the prophetic elders returned to the gates and stood guard.

These prophetic elders from within local Churches will once again actively stand guard at the gates (the spiritual point of entry) to their cities, controlling the very commerce (both material and spiritual) of that city, guarding against evil and inviting good. Cities will know boom or bust depending on the diligence or lack of diligence on the part of the citywide prophetic elders.

In addition, as prophetic elders in a city come together in unity, that city will also know revival as it had never known it before! Revival will also begin at the gates!

Revival will be the responsibility of the resident, citywide prophetic elders — not traveling evangelists. These great citywide revivals will produce incredible results as thousands will be saved. Consequently, there will be drug-free cities, crime-free cities, and cities with virtually no unemployment because the prophetic elders of that city persevered in unified prayer and intercession.

THREE

PROPHETIC ACCURACY

Some prophets will demonstrate nearly inconceivable accuracy in their dreams, visions, and prophecies

Modeling a totally new and intense level of predictive accuracy, the prophets will speak into many secular, non-religious situations — temporal situations not normally associated with prophetic ministry.

Nation after nation will be stirred, some responding with acclaim and accolades or others with prosecution and persecution. Regardless of the reaction, this new level of accuracy will establish the prophets as legitimate messengers of God among the nations — forever.

Propelled into new and uncharted areas of revelation, these prophetic trendsetters, these prophetic trailblazers, will rewrite the rules of prophetic ministry. This fearless "Star Trek" prophetic company will "go where no man has gone before" as they delve into new and unfamiliar areas of prophetic ministry, championing various causes over which God has made them responsible. They will be His spokespersons, declaring the will of God regarding many social issues.

41

Great will be the demand placed on some of these internationally used prophetic men and women, and whole populations will cheer them on.

Once again, as in Old Testament days, certain prophets will even know the troop movements of nations at war with other nations, thus thwarting the military plans of evil rulers. Because of these intrusions by the prophets — which will be perceived as meddling in national affairs – some nations will have bounties placed on the heads of certain prophets.

These bounty hunters, actually hired by certain hostile governments, will chase the prophets around the world, pursuing them with demonic tenacity. Blasted as troublemakers by some nations, God's prophets will be hailed by many other nations as true peacemakers and defenders of righteousness.

The nation of **Israel** will especially benefit from these highly accurate prophets who will patrol her borders, acting as watchmen and providing protection to her people. As a nation, Israel will have no choice but to accept and appreciate the role these legitimate prophets will play.

In **Israel** there will be a state dinner held in honor of the prophets, and a day of national recognition for the prophets will be proclaimed — a nationally televised event!

NEW ACCURATE PROPHETIC BOOKS

The 21st century will see the proliferation of many new prophetic books written by prophets. These will burst forth to the nations. Prophets who were not writers will become authors. Those who were writers will do even more writing.

The purpose of this new emphasis on writing will be to furnish nations with clear prophetic insight and direction, written strategies, and prophetic blueprints. These insightful books will become very popular, nearly replacing cassette tapes in some parts of the world.

More and more, short prophetic books and booklets will flood the Church, bringing much-needed direction and encouragement.

In them, changing weather patterns will be forecast, economic trends outlined, political upheaval predicted, and the location of revivals pinpointed.

These important prophetic manuals will be greatly valued for the advantage they will bring regarding the plan of God for various nations. Acting as spiritual maps, these books will be a valuable resource to the Church of the 21st century, providing much needed guidance and direction. These accurate prophetic books will also contain strong national rebukes — powerfully written judgments.

Although some in the Church will be uncomfortable with this new breed of books, these important writings will be translated into many languages and considered as very valuable, becoming part of personal libraries all over the world.

Prophets and apostles will join forces to co-author a number of these powerful texts as international prophetic and apostolic partnerships cooperate in many such projects.

As a major avenue to the nations, these very books will challenge and confront governments. God will serve notice to entire governments, stating in no uncertain terms His expectations for those nations. Blessings will be given and curses carried out depending on a nation's response to these powerful books.

NEW ACCURATE MISSIONARIES

Missionaries will especially benefit from these books as they outline what regions, countries, and cities God will target for moves of His precious Holy Spirit.

These missionaries will report that great accomplishments were made for the kingdom of God with unusual ease because they went where God was moving. Wasted time and wasted resources will be a thing of the past for missionaries around the world as these prophetic books greatly increase missionary endeavors and efficiency levels soar!

Finances will be no problem, and the old adage "where God guides, He provides" will be the war cry of this new company of true Spirit-led missionaries.

Specifically, numerous cities in the **United States** will see an invasion of these anointed missionaries. They will not have to travel to foreign soil to evangelize the lost. Numerous **United States** cities will be turned upside down as a result of home-grown, indigenous missionaries being directed to these inner city harvest fields. Tens of thousands of souls will be saved as whole neighborhoods are taken back from the devil. Jesus will be glorified!

NEW ACCURATE APOSTLES

Many apostles worldwide will also experience a new anointing to write.

The apostles of **England,** particularly, will come under great unction to write on the strategies God gives them for the universal Church. These, too, will be basically revelatory books, full of practical insights for Christians in all nations.

These international manuals will be quickly distributed worldwide, while other writers will use the Internet and the worldwide web to reach nations.

NEW ACCURATE PROPHETIC FACTS

A fact is something based in actuality — a truth, a reality; something irrefutable, undeniable. By definition a "fact" is the exact meaning of something.

The 21st century prophets will deliver facts, literal facts covering a wide variety of subjects. They will speak revelatory words having real substance — divinely inspired words based in actuality and truth.

Their prophecies, dreams, and visions will be exact, in detail, word-for-word, heavenly messages from God. Astonishing things will be shown the prophets. No subject, no issue, no person will be beyond the prophetic reach of their revelatory gifting.

The secret plans of men will be exposed by the Holy Spirit. Criminals will be arrested based partially on prophetic evidence revealing their guilt in illegal activities. Specifically, organized crime worldwide will feel the pinch of strong prophetic words levied against them through the prophets.

Cities will break free from attempts to prostitute their economies by organized crime. Prophecy after prophecy will warn cosmopolitan areas to intercede against organized crime. The battle over crime will be won through this intercessory prayer.

This new breed of prophet will operate regularly in a new prophetic accuracy based in undeniable truth, explicit detail, and incredible clarity. The nations of the world will not be able to mount an offensive against these prophets of God because of the accuracy they will display.

There will be no arguments given, no debates raised, no intellectual discussions forthcoming about whether or not the prophets' words are truly from God. God will use His prophets to convince and convict the nations!

Everyone will admit that the prophets are genuine, although not everyone will embrace their respect among the nations for one simple, irrefutable, inarguable reason — extraordinary prophetic accuracy.

SONS OF ISSACHAR

The skill and ability to properly discern the times — like the original sons of Issachar — will become a new trademark of the new millennium prophets. Specific dates and times will be revealed through prophecy, even pinpointing the very year, month, and even the very hour of certain events.

God will tell the prophets to go to specific places at specific times. Timing will become a major factor with the prophets, and God will sovereignly speak, telling His prophets when to go and when not to go. If He speaks, they will go, regardless of the price; but if He does not speak, they will learn to remain where they are until He does.

Specific geographical locations, including actual street addresses will be shown the prophets, telling them where to go and whom to see. Actual names of individuals will be spoken to the prophets, and they will travel worldwide as the result of this divine information, seeking out key individuals and delivering to them the word of the Lord.

A new, incredible accurate, precise, literal brand of God-breathed prophecy will fill the Church.

The words of the Samaritan woman will be repeated often around the world in response to this new level of prophetic accuracy: "Come, see a man who told me everything I've ever done."

Prophets will know the who, what, where, when, and why God's will for many. Some will accept, others will reject the word of the Lord.

FOUR

PROPHETIC EVANGELISM

*Prophets will preach the gospel with
signs and wonders following*

A new burden for the lost in the 21st century will give the prophets the appearance of being New Testament evangelists.

By breaking the prophetic mold they have grown accustomed to and stepping into new evangelistic venue of ministry, these prophets will witness scores of people healed and, more importantly, scores of people saved!

NEW TESTAMENT EVANGELISTS

This unfamiliar and uncomfortable leading for evangelism among the prophets will be a difficult transition for some to make, but it will produce tremendous results in lasting fruit. Prophets will soon discover that the primary mode through which signs and wonders will flow will be through their evangelistic messages in evangelistic services and largely directed to unsaved audiences.

Specifically, more unsaved people than saved people will be healed, and more miracles will be performed outside the Church than in the Church — all due to the obedience of these new evangelistic prophets. The collective heart of these worldwide prophets will be to see true conversions on a mass scale flood into the Church – and this they will see!

Companies of these evangelistic prophets will roam the earth, preaching the good news of the gospel of Jesus Christ as God marvelously and miraculously endorses their message. The great Commission of Jesus Christ will become a new and powerful mandate from heaven to the prophets.

PICKED UP AND PLUNKED DOWN

The supernatural dimension of true New Testament evangelism will be restored to the Church. There will be little time to waste, and the Holy Spirit, will move in unusual ways to reach the lost and dying of the world.

Like Philip, some will even be physically transported from one region to another by the Spirit God. Literally, men and women of God will be instantaneously picked up and plunked down as they are physically placed in other geographical locations by the hand of God to evangelize whole populations.

These types of supernatural gatherings will be Spirit-birthed, totally spontaneous, and virtually unplanned by human effort. These sovereign, anointed, evangelistic crusades, divinely organized and sovereignly orchestrated by God, will not necessarily be endorsed by all nations.

Before governments can shut them down, however, the meeting will conclude on their own. The new converts will go back to their homes to form new churches in their communities, and the prophetic evangelists will go to their next appointed location.

The Holy Spirit will continuously give His servants the advantage by keeping them one step ahead of certain hostile governments. It will be a great irritation to many nations when they discover what God have done as He moved in a mighty way right under their noses.

These impromptu supernatural campaigns will be like seeds that will grow into many churches. Underground churches of this kind will proliferate worldwide, and no man will receive credit for the amazing number of churches that will suddenly sprout. God will receive all the glory!

BABY BOOMERS

A 21st century "baby boom" of spiritual infants will show the nations that God is calling a people from the four corners of the earth. The sheer numbers of new converts ushered into the kingdom of God in this unorthodox style will cause many meetings to take on the appearance of being out of control.

Wonderfully wild, highly energetic, totally enthusiastic, virtually free of all religious restrictions, these new babes in Christ will affect the Church worldwide. What may seem at first to be out of control will only be the natural response of spiritual prisoners set free.

Thousands will be healed of AIDS and dance for joy. Thousand will be miraculously fed by God through divine intervention and will sing His praises. Healings, deliverances, mass water baptisms by the thousands, and miracles of unprecedented proportions will all contribute to this new release of emotion, thankfulness, and relief.

The worldwide Church will take on the appearance of a huge nursery filled with infants, all of whom will need the love and attention of the older Christians. For the 21st century, every Christian will have a ministry, and everyone will have a job to do. There will be a great need for spiritual " nursery workers" in Church.

THE WORD OF KNOWLEDGE RESTORED

All the gifts of the Spirit will experience a definite and dramatic increase in both frequency and intensity during the 21st century.

Specifically, the revelatory gifts of the Holy Spirit: the word of knowledge, the word of wisdom, and the discerning of spirits will proliferate worldwide. Of these three, the word of knowledge will become a particularly effective tool for evangelism.

This gift will provide specific, accurate, literal insight into people's lives — especially the lives of the unsaved.

Historically, in many Pentecostal circles, this gift was limited to identifying certain sicknesses, ailments, or physical injuries, and this will certainly continue to be one use of the gift. God will begin to cause this wonderful gift to branch out in many directions, however.

As the gift operates through His people, many will be converted. The world will be unable to deny the impact this fully restored gift of the Holy Spirit had on them.

FIVE

PROPHETIC WORSHIP

The prophets will revolutionize the way the Church worships.

A heavy, thick blanket of prophetic anointing will radically alter worship in the 21st century as prophets steer the Church into new levels of high praise to God.

PROPHETIC HIGH PRAISE

What will this new prophetic praise, this high praise, sound like? It will be much more than the typical "new song" and more than merely spontaneous simple choruses.

This new prophetic worship will be sharper and crisper with a clear prophetic edge to it. It will sound like the worship of heaven — literal high praises! Imagine, the actual praises of heaven filling the Church, catapulting worshippers to the very throne room of heaven!

Something new, something anointed, something prophetic will be unleashed upon the Church, and praise will become actual prophecy, inspired messages from God that the Church will sing

51

back to God. To experience 21st century praise and worship will be to experience prophecy – to experience inspired utterance!

As God fills the Church with His manifest presence, prophecy in the form of song will dominate worship. In direct response to His presence, worshippers will sing to God the very messages He places in their hearts. This exchange — this immediate returning of the very words, sentences, themes, and messages from God — will be the characteristic that makes this new level of praise so prophetic, so inspired.

Like all forms of prophecy, there will be a distinct message, a primary purpose in this new worship.

WORSHIP LEADERS WILL PROPHESY

As the 21st century prophets impart their anointing to others, many worship leaders will evolve into strong prophets in their own right. As hands are laid on these gifted vocalists and instrumentalists, every Church that has a worship leader will also have an in-house prophet — with both ministries found in the same person!

These prophets will use their instruments and their voices to prophesy over their pastors, to prophesy over the congregations they serve, to prophesy over their city, to prophesy against the kingdom of darkness, and to prophesy over nations! They will prophesy in song to new rhythms, new tempos, new melodies, new styles of music.

People will flock to churches early to get the best seats and to be in the permeating atmosphere of worship. No one will want to miss a single song, and the presence of the Lord will arrive very quickly, often on the first note.

THE PROPHETIC SHOUT

The prophetic "shout" will be reintroduced to the Church through these anointed, prophetic worship leaders. The loud praises of God and the high praises of God will be one in the same.

Worship of this nature will virtually pulverize the wickedness in high places over certain geographical regions.

PROPHETIC CHOIRS

A new prophetic anointing will come on entire choirs, and they will prophesy as one voice, filling the Church with prophetic praise.

Spontaneous praise will interrupt our pre-planned services, and churches will begin to sing in rounds, voices echoing off one another in perfect harmony.

Notre Dame and many other European cathedrals will be filled with this type of worship.

PROPHETIC NATIONAL ANTHEMS

New national anthems — sacred choral compositions of praise and worship God — will be sung by the nations. These songs, a mixture of prayer and praise, will stir the angels of heaven, causing them to come to the aid of nations under siege by the Devil.

One nation will write anthems for another, and an international Spirit of cooperation among worship leaders will augment free exchange of these prophetic anthems worldwide.

Nations such as **Nigeria, Angola, the Democratic Republic** of the **Congo, Namibia,** and other nations along for the western coast of **Africa** will break the hold of the devil over them through the use of such supernatural songs.

There will be an increase in prophetic warfare songs. These songs, written specifically to certain nations as new prophetic anthems will actually determine the future course of that country.

Other prophetic songs will be like lullabies from the Father, songs of safety and security from God to certain nations. Through these love songs, God will express His great care and concern for the nations.

The Scandinavian countries of **Norway, Finland, Sweden** will not be ignored by the prophets or their songs. Prophetic songs for specific Scandinavian countries will begin to soften the hearts of these people. These songs will prepare them for a powerful invasion of God. God will replace passivity, lethargy, and indifference toward the things of God with a new, white hot fervor.

KIDS EVERYWHERE

Kids choirs will spring up everywhere!

Powerful anointed kids will lead worship services. Groups of ten- to twelve-year-olds will bring churches to their knees in worship.

Tongues and interpretation of tongues will flow out of these kids. There will be miraculous musical accompaniment during worship even when there are no instruments being played or even available. The angels will assist their efforts.

INVENTIVE/CREATIVE PRAISE

Regarding praise and worship, the sky will be the limit for the 21st century! Inventive and creative forms of expression will break out on every front as the Church witnesses the introduction of new and unusual forms of worship brought in by the prophets.

Full-length Christian operas will make their way into churches and the secular world as well. Performers outside the Church will be jealous, envying what God has done as the level of artistic expression intimidates many of the world's seasoned artists.

Anointed plays with large casts will become a part of many worship services. Numerous skits and excellent dramas of every type will fill our Churches with new life. All the arts will take on a highly prophetic appearance as God uses them to speak to the Church and the world.

CREEDS, CHANTS, INSTRUMENTS

New levels of worship will birth new prophetic creeds. These will be new standardized prayers containing statements of faith similar to the ancient Apostles' Creed. Churches will set these new prayers or creeds to music, singing of their faith in God.

Also, new prophetic chants, rhythmic melodies, and canticle declarations will be introduced into worship. Whole congregations will stand in the presence of the Lord for hours and hours chanting back to God all His wonderful attributes. The glory of the Lord will fill these sanctuaries!

New musical instruments will be invented, further adding to this new unique sound of 21st century worship.

The world will no longer affect the worship of the Church; the Church will radically affect the music of the world. They will borrow from us; we will no longer borrow from them.

Specifically, France will introduce some of these new musical instruments to the Church as young, creative Christian inventors excite the Church with their gift of inventive genius.

REVIVAL PROCESSIONALS

Japan will contribute greatly to this new era of praise and worship in the Church by introducing her unique and exciting form of worship to the nations. Specifically, **Japan** will show the world how to organize huge outdoor processions. These great public marches of praise will be grand displays using banners, fireworks, floats, balloons, and even costumes!

Wave after massive wave of Japanese Christians in anointed marches will fill the streets giving God the glory. This phenomenon will spread worldwide!

Taiwan, which God has targeted for a great revival, will see several such revival marches. The hills will be alive with the sound of new music — loud, spontaneous, liberating worship! The Christian Church of **Taiwan** will explode with revival power affecting the nations around her.

The **United States** will send many Christians there to observe the miracles that will take place. Books containing photos of the creative miracles that are performed in **Taiwan** will circle the earth. Even the dead will be raised!

Also, Korean marchers will be invited to other nations to assist in their national processions.

The **Hawaiian Islands** of the United States will be visited by God, causing ancestral pride and cultural smugness to disappear. The people will rejoice before God their maker! **Hawaii** will become a hot bed of revolutionary praise and worship as new and distinct styles of worship abound, influencing nations and reviving the Church.

There will be a new supernatural and strategic significance to these islands. Their spiritual and military value will become of tremendous importance to the **United States** in the 21st century. They will become a sanctuary for prayer and fasting to the nations. This vacation mecca will become a spiritual mecca for many Christians.

Also, huge refugee camps will litter the **Hawaiian Islands** as displaced people pour in from Asian nations. All this will be part of a great plan — a divine scheme — and God will move powerfully with many dramatic conversions recorded.

The military presence on the islands will include an expansion of airport facilities, including many miles of additional runways both civilian and military. The civilian and military population of the **Hawaiian Islands** will also greatly increase.

SIX

PROPHETIC TRAINING

A new breed of teaching and training prophets will arise in the 21st century.

There will be more teaching prophets, more classroom prophets, more training prophets than ever before in the history of the Church.

HEADQUARTERS

Many different kinds of schools for the further training and releasing of thousands of anointed prophetic Christians will be birthed.

As much as prophets will fly to other lands, other lands will fly to the prophets as they set up ministering headquarters in their respective home lands. Enrollments will explode overnight in many of these schools with eager international student bodies, creating a true melting pot of Christianity.

MOBILE SCHOOLS

There will also be a new mobile prophetic school movement within the Church. Mobilized itinerant prophets will take their schools to the local churches, thus customizing the individual school to that specific church.

The **United States** will see a proliferation of this type of mobile prophet as they take their teaching techniques to the worldwide Church.

Indonesia will also host many such schools, thus affecting a very large area from Asia to Australia.

PROPHETIC CURRICULUMS

Prophets will develop new comprehensive, prophetic curriculums for the Church —complete courses of study on prophecy.

The demonstration of prophetic gifts or prophetic words will no longer be the mainstay of the prophets. They will become multi-dimensional men and women, prophetic teachers, laying sound, biblical prophetic foundations.

They will offer practical teachings of exactly how to function in prophecy within the very framework and infrastructure of the local churches they visit.

God's people will benefit greatly! Even some denominational churches will welcome the prophets and their new curriculums.

ALL KINDS OF SCHOOLS

Training centers, retreat centers, fasting centers, prayer centers, and worship centers will arise.

In the **United States, Oklahoma, Arkansas,** and **Florida** will be home for many such centers.

The New England states (**Maine, New Hampshire, Vermont, Massachusetts, Connecticut,** and **Rhode Island**) will be a teaching center for the worldwide Church.

God is going to breath upon New England once again, and a great revival will hit this region of the **United States.** Ezekiel's vision of the valley of dry bones will be fulfilled in New England, and new life will resurrect this region's spiritual life as the spirit of intellectualism is displaced by revival.

Even now God is telling His prophets to prophesy over New England, thus releasing God's power and presence over that region of the world.

SCHOOL DAYS, SCHOOL DAYS

Globally, nearly every local church will have some kind of in-house school attached to it. Prophets will have prophetic schools, apostles will have apostolic schools, and the five-fold ministers will become true trainers and equippers of the entire Church. No one will be left out.

Apostles will teach, prophets will teach, evangelists will teach, pastors will teach, and, of course, teachers will teach —and theological ignorance will be eradicated!

In the United States, the states of New York, Pennsylvania, and New Jersey will have many such prophetic/apostolic schools — all of which will be attached to local churches.

IMPARTATION MEETINGS

Powerful prophetic "such as I have" impartation meetings will explode throughout the Church worldwide. These meetings, sometimes lasting hours, will be devoted to the laying on of hands by mature prophets for instantaneous impartation of the gifts of the Spirit, especially prophetic gifts.

Consequently, Christians everywhere will experience an incredible increase in their ability to operate like the prophets who laid hands on them — many surpassing their prophetic predecessors in overall gifting.

Many prophets will be appreciated as much for the touch of their hand as for the prophetic words of their mouth.

Indonesia will specialize in demonstrating this awesome dynamic of impartation through the laying on of hands by qualified ministers. Many will travel to this nation and receive impartation of the power gifts: gifts of healing, working of miracles, and gift of faith.

SEVEN

PROPHETIC MONEY MANAGEMENT

*The prophets will help direct the wealth
of the wicked back to the righteous.*

The prophets will help direct the wealth of the wicked back
to the righteous.

What and where is this "wealth of the wicked" (Prov. 13:22) of
which the Bible speaks? How will the prophets obtain it, and, more
importantly, how will they direct and distribute it properly? These
are important questions that will be answered in the 21st century.

By definition, the "wealth of the wicked" is the combined
worldly assets of the unsaved — the totality of their commerce,
industry, and economy.

Traditionally, this worldly wealth is passed down through
inheritance from one generation to another. Consequently, these
same "wicked ones" keep their assets, using them for selfish,
self-preserving, and even evil purposes —and clearly not for the
purposes of God on the earth.

The prophets will change all of this! While the estates, assets,
goods, and cash of Christians remain in their respective families,

God will order that the gains of the sinners be transferred to the saints.

How will this supernatural transfer of funds take place? From where will this wealth come? Here is the word of the Lord on the subject.

DEBT-FREE LIVING

First, by removing long-term debt —the most common form of financial slavery — virtually hundreds of millions of dollars will become available to the universal Church. This will be a huge, passive transfer of funds.

Debt will die! As debt dies, the coffers of the wicked will no longer be filled by the righteous. Christians everywhere will enjoy a newfound freedom —a freedom from the yoke of debt.

Prophets will prophesy to the Church regarding all manner of financial matters with great boldness and conviction. By setting the example in their own lives, they will practice and preach that God's people should live debt free as much as possible.

Debt-free living for Christians will become the rule and not the exception in the 21st century. No longer will saint borrow from sinner. Instead, the Church will lend and not borrow!

SELF-EMPLOYMENT

Second, more and more Christians will become self-employed. This challenging way of life will not be for everyone, but it will work for many.

The prophets will direct many Christians into new and inventive businesses through prophecy. These new enterprises will be the vehicle for new wealth to be channeled into the universal Church —another blow against the wealth of the wicked.

Many Christians will inquire of the prophets, asking for specific instructions concerning the further investment of these funds and the prophets will oblige them, creating even greater wealth!

BANKING

Third, many major companies worldwide will be managed by Spirit-filled Christians. The banking and finance world will be secretly infiltrated by many of God's people.

Even now a clarion call is being issued to the Church to send young men and women into the fields of finance and banking, especially international banking. These highly educated and trained professionals will climb the ladder of corporate success quickly, constantly knowing the hand of God upon them while obeying His voice in business decisions. These decisions will positively affect the Church and keep literally thousands of people from financial bondage.

These new leaders will bring financial strategies into the Church, breaking generational histories of poverty. Many poor will become rich.

Many Churches will have tremendous bank accounts that will be made available to the prophets. Prophetic distribution of these funds will become commonplace as God directs these monies through the voices of His prophets.

GIFTS FROM THE UNGODLY

Fourth, prophetic men and women of God will channel large sums of money back into the Church. This is an awesome responsibility, but God will test the prophets and place great trust in them.

Through the prophets, millions of dollars will pour into the Church, but it will not be money they have necessarily earned. From where will this money come? What will be its source?

Supernaturally, God will bring this wealth from unsaved individuals who are moved upon to give. Large financial gifts will pour into the Church.

As a result, many third-world countries will see thousands of churches spring up – all paid with the wealth of the wicked!

Worldwide, many Churches will operate debt free as this miraculous influx of finances liberates them from the bondage of crippling debt.

International foundations will be set up as endowed institutions are structured solely to distribute this money back into the Church. These organizations will be overseen by the prophets who will listen to God to hear exactly where the funds are to go.

LAND AND PROPERTY

Fifth, the 21st century prophets will direct the Church to buy large tracts of land. This accumulation of land will be a great hedge against future economic volatility worldwide.

Also, many Churches will be given land through estates and inheritances. Do not be quick to sell! Keeping this land will prove to be the better decision in the years to come.

Specifically, cheap land in the states of **Mississippi, Alabama,** and **Louisiana** in the United States will appreciate rapidly during this new millennium. A prudent time to invest in land in this region would be now.

For many, individual wealth will grow too. Consequently, the churches they attend will prosper. Churches that once only dreamed of financing big projects will pay cash as prophetic offerings are taken and thousands of dollars are raised in an hour.

Airplanes will be purchased, whole city blocks bought, failed businesses will be auctioned off, and churches will buy them for pennies on the dollar. The economies of entire cities will be controlled by the churches in those same communities. All this for the funding of the gospel being preached to all nations!

FARMING

Sixth, God will give the prophets revelation into new agricultural techniques and inventions. Ground that was once cursed will be blessed. Thousands of acres of land once thought worthless will spring back to life for Christian farmers and growers.

God will bless churches with land so abundant that they will donate some of it back to their respective governments.

The Church will control whole food supplies. Christian businessmen will control the growing and distribution of food to the nations. Whoever controls the food will control the economy.

Money will pour into Christian food companies as nations spend their wealth to feed their people. More Christian millionaires will be made in the food industry — specifically, the growing and selling of crops and meats, etc. — than m any other single area of endeavor.

NEW INVENTIONS

Seventh, as a result of many Holy Spirit inspired inventions, Christians will hold more patents than any one single group. A new kind of inventive genius will begin to exhibit itself through the Church as many young people bring new inventions into the business world.

Specifically, God will use the next generation of believers in the areas of finance and banking, corporate management, architecture, engineering, and medicine.

Professionally skilled Christians will flood their respective job markets. They will be in high demand not only for their education and skill but also because of the presence of God that will rest heavily on them.

They will gain favor with man unlike any previous generation and will be promoted to places of authority and influence far beyond their years. They will be the Josephs of Egypt and the Davids of Israel for the 21st century.

MANY JOSEPHS OF ARIMATHEA

Also, the 21st century will be witness to some incredibly wealthy prophets. Some of the wealthiest men and women in the world will be this new breed of Josephs of Arimathea.

Righteous yet rich, they will not prostitute themselves with get-rich-quick schemes of any kind. These conservative servants will be experts at saving and not spending. Many of these prophets will live totally debt-free lives.

They will not prophesy any magic formulas nor any instant, overnight success investments, no get-rich-quick schemes. They will play key roles behind the scenes, doing their part in the plan of God to nations.

Like the original Joseph of Arimathea, they will have their eyes fixed on the kingdom of God and not on the wealth they possess. They will be truly selfless givers.

A DOMINO EFFECT

The **Episcopal church,** along with several other major mainline denominations in America, will cease to exist. Bankruptcy will be their sad demise, but it will be a timely death from God's perspective. He will use it for good, using these assets to further His kingdom.

The prophets will occupy many of these church buildings, reverently using these facilities for the glory of God. The attitude of the Episcopalian church will be quite good, even magnanimous by some standards. Very few within this one-time, great denomination will resist.

The sacred, holy soil upon which many of these beautiful sanctuaries were built will continue to be used for the glory of God —which was their intended purpose in the first place.

PARA-CHURCH ORGANIZATIONS

Numerous other established ministries outside the Church will fail during the new millennium. One such ministry will be the **Full Gospel Businessmen's Fellowship International.** This ministry, which had been a tremendous blessing around the world, unfortunately, will end in financial disgrace.

There will be a giant shifting of funds within the Church world —a new allocation of funds by the Lord of the Church. Parachurch organizations that once flourished will go on the decline while the life and vitality of the local church will increase.

Only those ministries closely associated with local churches will grow, especially evangelistic ministries. Trusted organizations, remnants left over from the 20th century, will transfer what money they have remaining to new and productive ministries. The old guard will at first resist this, but God will apply the pressure to make sure the money gets through.

Even leading Christian television networks will devote more resources than ever to worldwide evangelism.

One particular network, **The Christian Broadcasting Network,** will become radically evangelistic. Entire programs will consist of video from all over the world showing evangelistic meetings and actual miracles taking place right on camera. The excitement generated by these videos will be phenomenal, and many thousands of copies will be circulated by CBN. The finances will literally pour into this integral ministry , and they will sponsor many evangelists to the nations. CBN's finest hour is yet to come!

EIGHT

PROPHETIC JOY

A new, fresh, joy will come on the prophets worldwide.

Jesus said He wanted our joy to be full, and it will be precisely this sort of joy that the prophets of the new millennium demonstrate — a God-breathed, Holy Spirit joy.

DEEP ABIDING JOY

The prophets will walk in a deep abiding joy — something enduring, something supernatural.

This joy will be difficult to explain at first, difficult to put into words or to articulate in speech. It will be a joy that they are unaccustomed to, something unfamiliar, different, and distinct.

Yet, it will be a joy that unleashes incredible power — a catalyst for supernatural phenomenon. This power-packed joy will compensate for the sacrifice, rejection, pain, and suffering they will experience as they travel worldwide serving the Lord.

This joy of the Lord will be their strength, literally becoming the new trademark of the worldwide prophets of the 21st century.

SMILING THROUGH THE STORMS

These joyful 21st century prophets will be the most down-to-earth, accessible, relational men and women in the Church. Although they will take what they do for God very seriously, they will not take themselves seriously. They will be real.

They will be an unassuming bunch, a group of regular men and women —ordinary people with extraordinary gifts. When called upon by God, however, they will operate in great power and demonstration of the Spirit.

They will smile through the storms, laugh in the face of danger, and shout for joy at the great things God will do through them. They will be a happy troupe, with gladness in their hearts, their service to God giving them the most pleasure. They will delight in the Lord, bringing Him the glory.

GREAT ENCOURAGERS

These prophets will be known as great encouragers. In fact, this will be their ultimate legacy to the Church.

They will specialize in the healing of the complete individual — spirit, soul, and body. They will bring hope where there was no hope. They will snatch victory out of defeat, turning nearly impossible situations around through their strong prophetic gift.

They will spread joy wherever they go, depositing this gift of joy in churches around the world.

JOYFUL TRAVELING

Many prophets will experience geographical moves as the Holy Spirit relocates them nearer to metropolitan areas. Access to international airports will be a priority because the need to fly out quickly to the nations will be great.

Sudden, unexpected invitations in the early morning hours will awaken the prophets, and they will answer the call of God, traveling on a moment's notice to many lands. Even this strenuous demand on their gifting, however, will result in more joy being poured out upon them.

NINE

PROPHETIC GLORY

The manifest glory of the Lord will overshadow the prophets.

The glory will usher in miracles! God's thick, weighty glory —His actual physical presence, His wonder, His splendor — will accompany the prophets, validating and vindicating them wherever they go.

Translucent physical clouds of God's glory, physical rain showers, actual angelic choirs, and the unmistakable audible sound of the mighty, rushing wind of the Holy Spirit will be experienced by millions inside our sanctuaries as the prophets minister!

Churches will even smell the actual aroma of His sweet, sweet presence. Wherever the prophets go, things will happen — unorthodox things, wonderful things, things too marvelous to behold, and all for the glory of God!

A HOLY HUSH

The Church will learn to be still and know that God is God. Sacred times of total silence before God will not be uncommon as the glory of the Lord settles upon congregations around the world, capturing our corporate attention.

Twenty-four hour solemn assemblies will take place as God's glory fills our church sanctuaries and the people wait on God guided by the prophets.

The reverence of the original holy of holies will be experienced by the Church again. No one will dare speak; the glory of God will not permit it. And God will once again be feared among the nations.

WOUNDS WILL BE HEALED

The glory of God will produce permanent healing in many lives —physical, emotional, and spiritual wholeness. Specifically, the islands of the **Caribbean** will be host to many Christians seeking healing, and the glory will fall there in unprecedented ways.

The **Caribbean** Islands will experience a brief but dramatic time of divine judgment. God's glory will be revealed as He breaks the "party " spirit off the **Caribbean.**

These beautiful but wounded islands will become a holy place — a solemn place — and His glory will rest heavily upon this region of the world. God will bring healing to the people of these islands, and life there will never be the same.

BREAKING THE POWER OF VOODOO

The ancient evil of voodoo will die! How?

Voodoo has had a legal right to oppress this region of the world because of the sin of slavery. Slavery with all of its inhumanity and greed was never repented of by those who committed these horrible acts.

Consequently, the ground has been cursed, and the door opened for all types of evil. For hundreds of years the innocent blood of former slaves has cried out from the soil of the **Caribbean,** looking to be avenged.

The answer, however, lies not in vengeance but in repentance and the shed blood of Jesus Christ.

God will quickly — even suddenly — clean up the **Caribbean** once and for all as the Church stands in the gap, crying for forgiveness and redemption.

UNBEARABLE CONVICTION

All around the world —because of this awesome glory of the Lord — nearly unbearable conviction from the Holy Spirit will come to bear on the unsaved.

Four and five hours of repentance in a service will not be unusual for sinners and even for some who claim to be saved. True biblical conversion will once again be restored worldwide, and "saved" will once again mean "saved."

The Christian Church in **China** will help restore and model the reality of what it means to be truly converted.

A NEW MANDATE

Some major conferences will fail because over-zealous Christians will try to duplicate the spontaneous presence (glory) of God. Overall, organized conferences will decrease, and spontaneous, sovereign gatherings will increase worldwide.

A new mandate from heaven will rest upon the Church. It will be: minimum organization — maximum spontaneity, in order that the Church might learn to accommodate His glory!

European nations will host many successful unplanned, unprecedented "glory" gatherings that will specialize in healing and deliverance.

Yet, God warns the Church: "Do not merchandise My glory. Do not market My presence. I will not have it."

Consequently, video taping will not be allowed in some of these holy gatherings.

TEN

PROPHETIC BIRTHS

*Many major, worldwide prophetic
ministries will be birthed in a day.*

The gestation period for the prophets will end, and there will be many prophetic births — sudden births, instant births worldwide!

Many unknown prophets, those formerly held in reserve by God for release at a later time, will be catapulted into national prominence in a day. Suddenly, instantly, and miraculously, prophetic organizations will be born —and the world will take notice.

UNPRECEDENTED MEDIA COVERAGE

Overnight press coverage of the prophets' activities and exploits will promote these servants in an instant. You will see them on morning TV shows, read their interviews in magazines and newspapers, and hear their voices over radio. The media coverage will be unprecedented and free!

The prophets will show the world video tapes of people walking on water — some of the most amazing video to ever be shown on TV.

Even those raised from the dead will give their personal testimony on the air — and people will marvel at the power of God!

Some news stations will actually line up to cover the prophets — such will be the popularity of their ministries.

Through God's power, the prophets will change the courses of rivers, natural disasters will be averted, and whole weather patterns will be altered by their words. All this will capture the attention of the nations and bring glory to God.

This display of supernatural demonstration, however, will also cause panic and fear among some.

PROPHETIC ROYALTY

A male member of a prominent royal family will begin his own prophetic ministry — a prophet in his own right. He will travel to **Jerusalem** and speak prophetically over that holy city.

This gentile, skilled statesman, ambassador, and diplomat will play a major role in the political activities of Israel.

ELEVEN

PROPHETIC CATHOLICS

*An awesome army of Catholic prophets
will storm the gates of hell.*

The Roman Catholic Church will see a worldwide proliferation of legitimate prophets arise from her ranks during the 21st century.

God says, "Do not count the Catholics out!" These Catholic prophets, classic late bloomers, will be trained outside the Catholic Church and then will return to bring out those who will come.

A GREAT EXODUS

Led by this new breed of Catholic prophet, a great exodus will substantially decrease the overall size of the Catholic Church, leaving only diehard adherents of this denomination to resist these changes.

The irony is clear. The very prophets God raises up to renew the Catholic Church will be categorically rejected by its leadership. Despite their best efforts, these prophetic men and women will effect no lasting change among the Catholic hierarchy, but the laity of the Catholic Church will respond by the millions!

CATHOLIC PROPHETS

In spite of severe persecution by fellow Catholics, Catholic prophets will operate in a new prophetic audacity never before seen by Christendom. These empowered lay leaders will birth many small groups — some of which will grow into great churches in their own right.

Sadly, however, the Catholic Church will condemn such groups, ultimately issuing orders of excommunication to many of them. This threat, however, will not stop the flood of prophetic activity from rising to new heights.

Eventually, Catholic and Protestant prophets will model a new unity in the Spirit, working together side by side. The release of prophetic power will be exponential!

As a result of this prophetic awakening among the Catholics of the world, Rome-based Catholic leadership will come under intense scrutiny by many of its followers.

Some of the most loyal Catholics, specifically European and Latin American Catholics, will revolt. Rome's authority will be cut by two-thirds of what it is now.

ROME'S DANGEROUS PATH

During this time of spiritual instability within the Catholic Church, Rome will take on a new and dangerous political appearance.

A concerted but misguided political effort from high-ranking church officials will take the Catholic Church down a self-destructive path. She will cease to be a strong spiritual voice for Christianity and will become a weak, insipid political voice.

Consequently, Rome will have little spiritual impact on her followers. Her glory days behind her, Rome will resort to political game playing, maintaining only the outward appearance of a once-healthy Christian denomination.

PART TWO

Predictions for the Nations

AFGHANISTAN & IRAN
Judgments of God

T he national borders of Afghanistan and Iran will change drastically, even permanently, as their sovereignty is compromised through war with neighboring nations. These nations will also suffer internal strife and violent civil unrest within their respective borders as their populations revolt.

GOD'S JUDGMENTS UNLEASHED

God's judgments — although delayed for years because of His great mercies — will finally be unleashed.

The heavens will withhold the rains, and parts of this region will see no rain for ten years. Mighty rivers will dry up, and water supplies will fall critically low — the lowest ever.

For the very few who call upon the Lord for salvation, there will be divine protection and provision for them. Some will even be allowed to leave — a rare opportunity to escape persecution and death.

Major Christian relief organizations will set up permanent new cities for these refugees.

AN ANGEL OF MERCY

Russia will cooperate with the West in this huge humanitarian effort.

As a nation, Russia will show more mercy to these people than ever imagined, even risking the loss of political advantage to do so.

The heart of Russia will be enlarged, and many nations will be pleasantly surprised at her new nature — a merciful and compassionate nation willing to help and not hurt other nations.

AFRICA

The Beginning of Sorrows

In the natural realm, huge volcanoes will shake Africa, and islands will literally sink off her coasts.

In the spiritual realm, it will be the same.

African nations will continue to experience birth pangs. Nation after nation will wrestle with its past, trying to break free from ancient curses (some self-imposed) along with tribal hatred and political upheaval.

There will be no quick and easy solutions for this troubled continent.

EXTRACTING A PEOPLE FOR GOD'S KINGDOM

Still, there is hope for the Church in Africa.

What will God do?

Generally, God will extract a people from out of a people — a godly minority. This process will be similar to the process used to extract olive oil from the olive.

God will apply great pressure to this continent. This divine pressure will cause the earth to shake and quake, its crust to crack. These rumblings will cause His Church to grow!

All this pressure will bring out the best in His people, creating some of the purest, most anointed Christians in the kingdom.

Africa will demonstrate true holiness to the world.

ASIA MINOR

New Beginnings

A supernatural door of evangelism to Asia Minor will be opened wide, and prophets will pour in from the West. Outdoor meetings will attract tens of thousands.

Twenty-first century prophets will travel to **Kazakhstan, Uzbekistan, Turkey, Azerbaydzhan, Afghanistan, Pakistan, Tadzhikistan,** and other surrounding nations in great numbers. These apostolic/prophetic pioneers will establish many churches in the homes of new converts.

HIGH RISK — HIGH YIELD

Although there will many dangers associated with ministering in these countries, God will protect His servants in this high risk, high yield field for ministry. Even as war breaks out in this region, the Church of Jesus Christ will flourish.

God will sovereignly send His workers into this volatile vineyard, but the rewards will outweigh the dangers.

Let this serve as a warning to those who would venture into these countries in a casual manner: Unless God sends you, do not go!

There will be no room for observers or the curious in these nations of Asia Minor. Only well-trained, seasoned, and Spirit-led men and women need apply.

The Lord will direct many to these harvest fields, using dreams and visions to guide them specifically to certain cities He has sovereignly selected.

God says to these nations, "You are Mine — all of you."

CANADA

Leadership Among the Nations

Central and Western Canada will see a great influx of new peoples, especially Orientals from all over the world — some even from unexpected places.

Consequently, great opportunities for evangelism will arise, and churches will become virtually multi-ethnic overnight. Mega churches will proliferate.

This unusual "population explosion" due to relaxed immigration policies will add to the strength and diversity of Canadian life and especially to the Church of Jesus Christ.

DEFEATING RACISM

At first, many of these oriental converts will isolate themselves in churches of their own nationality or race.

There will be resistance to these new peoples from many Canadian nationals, but the Canadian churches will gladly welcome these new brothers and sisters. Eventually, all races will worship together, and this subtle form of racism will be defeated.

Many immigrants will return to their homelands with the message of the gospel in their hearts.

Canadian pastors will establish schools to train these missionaries as they return home — some to stay permanently, others temporarily.

A CLEAR DESTINY

Canada's highest government offices will be visited by the Prophets.

At the request of Canadian officials, these prophets will address governing bodies of politicians, delivering the word of the Lord to Canada on several occasions.

Hard economic times will soften Canada's heart and allow the prophets access to this nation as never before in her history.

As a nation, Canada will learn to depend on God and God alone as a spirit of independence and self-sufficiency disappears.

Canada's role in international politics will increase, and she will be a trusted friend to many less fortunate nations.

Canada has a clear and definable destiny to fulfill, and God will use her mightily.

CHINA

A Cleansing

The precious people of China — not necessarily their government or their leaders — will let out a collective victorious shout! It will be a spiritual outcry so deafening that the government of China will be forced to listen and cooperate with the changing times.

DELIVERED FROM COMMUNISM

Communism will slowly crumble. The Chinese people will be delivered from the tyrannical rule of her political leaders.

The Christian Church will explode! In the wake of this somewhat violent transformation, a fledgling democratic movement will eventually overtake the nation, and Christian leaders will occupy prominent positions in government.

China will become known as the land of liberty in the Far East, politically and religiously — quite the opposite of its present reputation.

DIVINE PRESSURE

China's massive national turnaround will happen through tremendous divine pressure.

China will be hemmed in by the hand God. She will not be permitted to dominate or dictate to other nations, although she will try to exert her influence many times.

Supernaturally frustrated, China's attempt to disrupt the balance of power among the nations will fail. China will threaten her neighbors with war only to find that domestic issues distracted her attention from her military endeavors.

A strong consideration of nations will hold her in check militarily and economically. Like a bully, China will try to expand her borders but without permanent success.

DOCTRINAL CLARITY

Finally, a strong connection between the Christians churches in **Russia** and **Korea** will help to establish the Christian Church in China, bringing much needed doctrinal clarity.

CUBA

From Death Will Come Life

Despite major internal upheaval, Cuba will remain a unified sovereign nation, becoming a close working partner with the **United States.**

Her military strength will nearly disappear. The **United States** will become her protector as America reaches out to Cuba as a brother would to a little brother .

A CHRISTIAN NATION

Eventually, Cuba will be a strong Christian nation in her own right with unusual miracles to report.

In her infancy as a Christian nation, Cuba will experience many internal attempts to undermine her Christian progress, but these will all fail.

Many of the cults from America will try but fail in their efforts to pollute the spiritual climate of Cuba.

Cuban missionaries will burn with revival fire, even igniting revival fires in the **United States, Canada,** and **Africa.**

EASTERN EUROPE — WESTERN ASIA

A Fresh Start

T he general region of Eastern Europe and Western Asia will literally explode with Holy Spirit power.

Spiritually speaking, Eastern Europe will now influence Western Europe. The current of God's river will change direction, and revival will flow backward into Europe from the east.

NEW DISCOVERIES

New discoveries of oil and mineral wealth will be found and will become a blessing from God for the years of suffering and poverty the peoples of this region experienced.

Also, many American ministries will have strong ties to this region.

A HOLY SPIRIT EXPLOSION

God will cause language barriers to fall on this Euro-Asian border.

Supernaturally, God will cause ministers from other nations to speak the native languages of the diverse countries. Translators will be out of business as the gifts of the Holy Spirit explode on the scene. Especially the gift of various kinds of tongues.

Incredible open visions of heaven will be seen by the Christians of this region, and many legitimate seers will be raised up within the Christian Church.

This area will also be a place ripe with lying signs and wonders. Satan will do His best to counterfeit the genuine outpouring of God's Spirit. There will be a need for true discernment among Christian leaders.

Some of the harshest winter weather ever will not slow down the pace of the Church in this region. A tremendous growth rate in the Christian Church will be recorded.

EGYPT
Sadness Then Gladness

The nation of Egypt will experience both severe judgment from God and incredible blessing from God.

God says, "I deeply love Egypt, My lost daughter, but I discipline those I love. "

RAIN FROM HEAVEN

Egypt will be forced to declare national bankruptcy as her currency becomes worthless. Her entire economy will be restructured with the help of outside experts. This national embarrassment, however, will save the Egyptian people from starvation as years of drought ravage her fields.

Simultaneously, a great revival in the Christian Church will shake Egypt to its core.

Eventually, as the blessing of God returns to her, Egypt will see supernatural, physical rains from heaven, and her deserts will spring forth into song! During that time, more precipitation will fall on Egypt than has ever been previously recorded.

This unprecedented amount of rain will usher in a new era of this barren nation. Tens of thousands of acres of lush, green crops will mean ultimate blessing and prosperity for her. She will become a breadbasket, exporting food to her neighbors.

STABBED IN THE BACK

The Lord issues this prophetic warning to Egypt and says, "Do not turn your back on Libya." Like a wounded animal looking for an easy meal, **Libya** will suddenly and swiftly attack Egypt at night when the people least expect it.

Using the excuse of having no food or water for her people, **Libya** will claim she is fighting for survival. In truth, she is looking to destroy her neighbor out of pride and arrogance.

Libya's real motivation will be the complete dominance of this entire region of the world. When **Libya** talks of permanent peace among Arab nations, let all the nations of the Middle East beware! Egypt, backed militarily by **Israel** and the navy of the **United States**, will prevail. The entire conflict will last only a week.

Although secret promises will be made to **Libya** by other Arab allies, no other Arab nations will join **Libya** in this war. Isolated and alone, **Libya** will retreat like a dog with its tail between its legs.

EGYPT AND THE UNITED STATES

The relationship between Egypt and the **United States** will grow stronger, and these two nations will become true friends.

On either side of the Suez canal, hundreds of American ships will line up to unload their goods. There will not be enough space to dock them all. Military and commercial vessels will bring a constant supply of military hardware and civilian necessities to Egypt.

ENGLAND
A Preparer of the Church

E ngland will become a great "exporter" to the world-wide Christian Church. She will export a new breed of apostles, a new model of preachers, and an army of women evangelists.

A HEALING ANOINTING

Unusual healings will take place in cities all across England. Specific cities will be known as healing centers for specific diseases. Many people will be healed on their way to these geographical locations — before they even arrive!

Incredible supernatural demonstrations of God's power will free many from lifelong ailments in an instant, and people from around the world will come to drink of these healing waters made available by a loving, caring God.

As this healing anointing spreads, city after city will witness inconceivable, unimaginable, divine healings that will set the standard for power evangelism around the world. As a result, these cities will birth a new breed of power evangelists, many of them women.

These highly prophetic women will take this healing anointing throughout **Europe** and **Asia,** then around the world! Specifically, **France, Belgium, The Netherlands, Russia, Romania, Hungary, Poland,** and **the Czech Republic** will benefit from the overflow of this English revival.

STANDING GUARD

As England is sovereignly blessed within her borders, foreign powers outside her borders will rise up against her .

England will be targeted by non-Christian nations, especially

Islamic nations, who will push her to the brink of war. Some of her former allies, however, will stand by and mock her.

In the face this assault, Christians from around the world will unite in intercession, and England will be spared. Her biggest ally of all, the **United States,** will stand faithfully by her side militarily, politically, and spiritually.

As foreign tensions mount, a group of valuable "watchman" type prophets will stand guard over England, issuing accurate prophetic warnings to the nation. Even now God is issuing such a warning against a new insidious form of terrorism that will strike against England's population.

God says to England, "Guard yourself against foreign terrorism, especially in the cities of your northeastern coast. Don't be fooled by the past. Nations who claim to be your friends will prove otherwise."

THE HAND OF GOD

Economically, England will enter the 21st century stronger than ever. When other allies are not doing well economically, she will prosper. This will be a supernatural sign from God.

National illnesses — physical ailments that have gone unchecked for years —will suddenly decrease as God's mercy falls on England. Her national birth-rate will increase dramatically —a blessing from God.

Even new oil reserves will be discovered off her shores. Finally, God will clean up her political process, eliminating corruption and greed, making England an example for other nations to follow.

Clearly, the hand of God will be on England in a special way. She must remember to whom much is given, much will be required.

ETHIOPIA
Mercy and Grace

A s a result of a sovereign act of God, Ethiopia will become a Christian nation. Like a lighthouse she will pierce the darkness of that entire region.

God will supernaturally appoint a new government and give the nation a new name. Her new name will mean "Grace."

The country will take on a new national beauty, which will be the product of a divine visitation, transforming her appearance. She will experience a renaissance of her former days and her glory .

A reflection of God will be seen by other nations.

A THREESOME

Although defenseless in many ways, Ethiopia will experience God as her protector. Nations that rise up against Ethiopia to invade her will be defeated as they are confused and routed by Almighty God.

Israel will improve her relations with this new Ethiopia, and along with the **United States** will contract to feed her and protect her for a season.

A strong military alliance between the United States and Ethiopia will play a key role in keeping the peace in this region for years to come.

This military presence will benefit the kingdom of God as Christian missionaries venture into this region, bringing the glad tidings to the lost. It will be a marvelous harvest of souls.

A FLOURISHING ECONOMY

Ethiopia's economy will not only stabilize but will eventually flourish.

Untapped natural resources will bring blessing to her as foreign investment and management of these resources add to her national healing.

Her borders will expand to include territory taken from her, and her latter days will be blessed more than her former days. Truly, Ethiopia will be blessed among nations.

FRANCE
Destiny Delayed

Sadly, France will refuse to assume her responsibilities in the 21st century as expected. Even now God is asking, "Where is France, My wayward child?"

The good news is: There will be no judgments brought against France by God. He will show the French nation His mercy , but France will essentially shoot herself in the foot.

SELFISH DECISIONS

Eventually, France will drop out of the United Nations, citing philosophical differences with other nations. This unwise isolationist policy will have no real lasting effect, although her currency will be permanently weakened as a result.

France will also make promises she cannot keep, and nations in the European community will lose confidence in her.

Europe will turn its back on France during her time of need as her selfish ways are exposed.

The **United States,** however, will respond to her old ally. When other nations say, "No!" America will say, "Yes!"

Although embarrassing to France, this proud nation will be forced to take a loan from the United States to help stabilize her crumbling economy.

A NEW OPEN DOOR POLICY

In the midst of all this internal strife, a powerful anointed minority of French apostles and prophets will have a great impact on Europe, especially the Scandinavian countries.

In spite of God's disappointment with her, France will still be a refuge for many persecuted believers from around the world. A new national sense of hospitality will come upon France, and she will adopt a new open door policy of which God will take full advantage.

FRENCH APOSTLES

The opportunity afforded foreign missionaries in France, however, will change for the worse. A new more strict policy will severely limit the ability of missionaries to evangelize this nation.

God, however, will provide more than enough workers from within France, and His Church will be built. Several national apostolic figures will provide strong leadership — and the Church will be saved. These visionaries will guide France through a very difficult time brought on by her own shortsightedness.

GERMANY
Prophetic Power

Germany will experience an incredible revival with supernatural fireworks in a way she has never seen. This will especially be true concerning angelic visitations.

This move of God will be 100 times more powerful than anything seen in the 20th century as mighty angels pour out unimaginable signs and wonders on her people. In honor of this unprecedented and undeniable reawakening, a new German holiday will be declared and huge national marches will be held —all for the glory of God!

Germany will never be the same!

REVIVAL AND REVOLUTION

Satan, the arch enemy of the Bride of Christ, will not sit idly by and allow this to happen. Aware of the importance of Germany in the last days, Satan will launch a strong counterattack —a hell-borne challenge against God's people.

Germany will experience both revival and revolution — one sent from heaven, the other sent from hell. Because of this nation's strategic geographical and spiritual importance in Europe, Germany —the target of Satan's fury —will come under fire again with a preemptive strike meant to paralyze her and keep her inwardly focused.

A NEW NAZI SPIRIT

Simultaneous to this wonderful revival, a well-financed attempt to undermine Germany's strong democracy will take place. A small, rich minority will attempt to raise a new flag over Germany.

This evil humanistic faction will attempt to assert the primacy of fallen man, but this assault will be short lived.Civil unrest resulting from a new Nazi spirit will form an even more demonic confederacy with the spirit of Islam.

Although this will be the devil's supreme attempt to thwart God's plans for Germany and her neighbors, it will ultimately fail. Instead, Germany will unite as never before in her history as a single-minded Christian nation.

A MODEL NATION

As a result of spiritual revival, Germany's leadership role among other Christian nations will increase. This once agnostic nation will emerge as a major launching pad for Christian missionaries around the world.

Many countries will copy the pattern established by Germany, both politically and spiritually, as she becomes a model nation —an example of humility and service to God.

The spiritual children of this great revival in Germany will be a host of power prophets. These anointed German ambassadors will travel the world, bringing revival to many nations.

South Africa will especially benefit from Germany's new prophetic thrust, and signs and wonders will accompany their message.

CONFUSION FROM THE CULTS

A second type of revolt will coincide with the political upheaval in Germany. The cults will target this nation and cause great confusion in the Church.

Christians everywhere will be mobilized to pray for Germany, especially that Bible teachers and pastors be raised up to feed and protect the sheep.

In spite of the civil unrest and spiritual attack of the devil, Germany will emerge as a united Christian nation, eager to do the will of God. Germany will become the second greatest money giver to the worldwide Christian Church.

THE MESSIANIC MOVEMENT

German Jews will not be able to dispute the power of this great heaven-sent revival, and many will be saved.

Globally, this German revival will have a profound effect on the messianic movement, especially in **Israel.**

Eventually, this worldwide messianic movement will fade away, having served its purpose. Jew and Gentile will blend together as one, worshiping side by side.

A NEW BREED OF APOSTLES

Another result of this revival will be a new breed of German apostles who will walk in true apostolic authority and power throughout the world.

German newspapers owned by Jewish believers will report the apostles' exploits, providing many photographs as proof. Whole editions will advertise the miracles they perform both outside and inside Germany.

INDIA
Kids, Kids, Kids!

I n India God will mobilize thousands of young people A strong evangelistic and prophetic army of kids will arise out of India. They will sweep north, touching those nations where the door to the gospel has been closed for years.

These young soldiers will also move in a strong deliverance ministry, literally cleaning out whole regions of evil spirits as they operate in a new spiritual authority.

Schools will spring up all over India to train these young warriors in the things of God.

Young people from all over the world will travel to India. There will be a mighty move of God directed specifically at young people — a kid's revival!

CHINA AND INDIA AT ODDS

India and China will clash heads, but it will not be a fight to the finish. This brief military incident will have strong international repercussions and will make neighboring nations nervous.

Fortunately, it will be settled through the intervention of other nations, especially England and the United States.

Both India and China will retreat with a ringing in their ears but no major injuries. Both nations will realize the consequences of their actions would be counterproductive to their national interests. There will be no winner in this big non-event. This non-nuclear spat will fizzle out, and the world will collectively sigh with relief.

INDONESIA
Expect the Unexpected

The many islands of Indonesia will be another center of great spiritual awakening, and nearly unbelievable miracles will be reported. Signs and wonders will abound, and God will vindicate His servants with demonstrations of the supernatural never before seen.

Martyrdom, however, will not be uncommon there. Many will die for their faith.

SHAKING OVER AND UNDER

God will shake not only the heavens over Indonesia, but He will shake the earth under her as well.

God will move mountains -- literal mountains. A physical, natural mountain will be moved by the hand of God.

When mountains tremble at the sound of His name, Indonesia will experience a further release of the Spirit of God upon her. The nation will buzz with testimony after testimony of miracles, signs, wonders — even the raising of the dead.

Although government agencies will try to keep these reports censored, video after video will find their way out from this corner of the world.

Indonesia, more than almost any other region of the world, will experience the physical glory of the Lord — glory clouds by day and pillars of fire by night!

IRELAND & NORTHERN IRELAND
Healing, Wholeness, and Happiness

In this troubled comer of the world, God will work perhaps one of His greatest miracles!

The masterful, yet evil diversion of the devil that has kept this region smoldering in hatred, bitterness, and resentment will finally be exposed, and mercy drops will fall.

The battle for men's souls can and will be won!

LAUGHING TOGETHER AGAIN

Like long lost brothers who have been supernaturally reunited, Ireland and Northern Ireland will laugh together again. It will not be a nervous or artificial or phony laugh. Instead, brothers will share laughter from deep down inside. It will be a laughter of release from centuries of tension and strife.

Even the soil, the physical ground, will sigh a sigh of relief —such will be the deliverance over this people. The awful physical, emotional, and spiritual wound will finally be healed by the supernatural hand of God.

The history of tribal violence with its lust for bloodshed and its insatiable hunger for death will come to an end. This ancient demon will rear its ugly head no more.

The Son of righteousness will arise with healing in His wings. God will exercise His great jealousy over this region and will ransom it for the kingdom of God.

Get ready, for it will happen suddenly!

RAIN FOR A DRY PEOPLE

Ireland will experience an unpredictable chain of events —half meteorological and half supernatural —that will suddenly awaken this land.

Like torrential showers, God's Spirit will rain down upon this spiritually dry people. Revival will break out in the countryside and in the cities —among the rich and the poor, as well as with Catholics and Protestants.

Churches will overflow with converts, and people will literally run to churches to experience repentance and salvation. Many ministers will be overwhelmed and will flee, hoping to escape this wonderful, yet terrible revival.

God will not be limited, and He will shake the established religious order of this land. It will be everything the people had hoped for and everything they had feared.

Names and titles, denominations and organizations will take a back seat to this wonderful —yet seemingly out-of-control-revival. Even Ireland's government officials will publicly acknowledge this incredible manifestation of the Holy Spirit. It will be undeniable.

A drastic increase in physical rainfall over this region will signify an increased outpouring of God's Spirit.

This will be a healing rainfall and a cleansing downpour upon the people. God will cleanse the land both physically and spiritually as physical rains and spiritual rains fall from the heavens simultaneously.

Streams and rivers will deepen and widen, overflowing their banks, as their waters announce this unprecedented visitation from God.

God says to Ireland, "Look up, for your redemption draws nigh."

SUPERNATURAL PEACE

God's promise for Ireland is that all things will become new. She will have a fresh start like that of springtime.

God will stamp newness and freshness all over Ireland and Northern

Ireland. Such will be the magnificent release of His love to them. Love, forgiveness, healing, and reconciliation will flow in this land.

Ireland will have one people, one government, one economy, one currency, one goal, one future. All will become as it was meant to be.

The devil will go down in defeat, and mighty angels will be flying back and forth over Ireland and Northern Ireland, crying, "Peace, peace, peace!"

And there will be peace; supernatural peace, permanent peace —the peace that surpasses all human understanding. Somehow —supernaturally, sovereignly, mysteriously, and suddenly —all the internal feuding will end.

The unprecedented ceasing of old hostilities will announce the arrival of the Prince of Peace. None other than the Prince of Life, Jesus Christ Himself, will arrive to visit this formerly troubled land, bringing lasting peace where there has been no peace.

AN ARMY OF YOUNG EVANGELISTS

Consequently, a massive revival among Ireland's very young people will take place. This sudden outbreak of Holy Spirit revival fire will cover the land even affecting **Scotland.**

A second target group, slightly older than the first, the 20-30 year old group, will also see a tremendous move of God. Married couples will flood into churches in huge numbers as God redeems their hearts. They will cease from their pursuit of material things and run hard after spiritual things.

Many missionaries will emerge from this move of God. With their original destiny in God realized, many converts —single and married —will join the army of evangelists that God will raise up. They will take the gospel to many lands.

ISLAND & ISLAND NATIONS
Awakening

Many islands and island nations worldwide will be powerfully visited by God.

Deemed insignificant and nonstrategic by many, God will take personal pleasure in blessing these tiny dots on the map — all to His glory! These islands and island nations will take the lead, spearheading new and powerful moves of God.

God will show the world He is "no respecter of persons" (Acts 10:34).

REVIVAL FIRE!

Nations like **Taiwan, Cuba, Trinidad, Japan, Madagascar, the Philippines, Indonesia, the Greek Isles,** and **New Zealand** will feel God's mighty hand pressed heavily on them. Unexplainable phenomenon will testify of this visitation from heaven. In some cases it will be a prolonged visitation much envied by others.

Island chains like the **Hawaiian Islands,** the islands of the **Caribbean,** even Eskimo populations along the Aleutians will be visited by the Holy Spirit.

Individual islands like **Tahiti, Corsica, Sardinia,** and **the Falklands** will also experience the fire of revival with the glory of God visibly descending on them as never before in their history!

HOLY SPIRIT MARINES

A special corps of ministers, a kind of Holy Spirit Marines, will specialize in invading these island nations. Wave after wave of anointed prophets will storm these beaches, retaking the ground lost to previous spiritual conflicts.

Already, God is placing His strategies in apostolic and prophetic ministers for these very nations. Although tiny in size, these isolated islands will see God do marvelous things.

ISRAEL
Troubling Times

Jesus said repeatedly to beware of false prophets.
This stern warning will especially apply to Israel in the 21st century. Many false prophets will arise out of this nation as a kind of prophetic frenzy will take over.

These false movements, hastily initiated by man and not the Holy Spirit, will be characterized by over-zealous, carnal, impatient, self-serving liars.

HEADQUARTERED IN ISRAEL

These self-proclaiming (false) prophets will come from all over the world to set up their "international headquarters" in Israel. Eventually, this unwelcome influx of deceptive men and women will become a national embarrassment — but not until the real damage is done.

These false prophets will be without accountability, answering to no one. Many of these rogue prophetic novices will not understand true prophetic ministry and will set themselves up for future spiritual disasters as they are sucked into this prophetic cesspool in Israel.

Essentially self-promoting men, driven by their egos, will lust for premature advancement and success for their ministries, paying a tragically high price for their so-called success. They will ruin themselves and many followers around them.

A PROUD, SUPERIOR SPIRIT

These false prophets will be an untested and immature bunch — prophesying to areas in which they have no true revelation or authority. Overall, they will do much harm!

At first, they will gain a wide audience as they play on the fearful emotions of God's gullible people. They will do much damage to the good name of legitimate prophets through the misuse of alleged prophetic gifts they falsely claim to possess.

This vindictive and overextended prophetic crowd will target anyone who disagrees with them, thus isolating themselves from the global community of true and tested prophets. They will operate in a negative, proud, superior spirit that will be counterproductive to the cause of Christ and will not fully realize "what spirit they are of."

BE WARNED!

It will become prudent to avoid any and all contact with this unrestrained, destructive false prophetic mob. Be warned now about this type of false Christian/Jewish prophet coming out of Israel.

Don't read their magazines, don't purchase their tapes, don't travel to their conferences, don't get caught up in the frenzy. They will be false prophets, and they will be dangerous — very dangerous!

In spite of this and other similar warnings, the Jewish population of Israel will buy into much of what these deceptive and error-filled prophetic ministers spew out to the nations.

Pray for Israel. She will need it!

ISRAEL AND THE UNITED NATIONS

Deception in the political arena will also affect the nation of Israel. Israel and the **United Nations** will collaborate on several projects that will appear humanitarian, benevolent and innocent to the untrained eye. Many nations will praise Israel for her unselfishness and generosity.

All that glitters, however, is not gold.

Israel will attempt to deceive other nations and disrupt the balance of power in the **Middle East.** God will not allow her to gain the advantage she wants and will resist Israel.

These deceptive attempts to control other nations will fail, and Israel will be confined to much smaller national boundaries than she would have wanted. Deals will be struck, promises made, gifts exchanged, but God knows best. He will not allow Israel to grow too big too soon. Israel will learn patience as she learns to lean on Almighty God and not her political and military might.

Beware when Israel and the **United Nations** unite. No matter how good it looks from the outside nor how noble the cause may appear, no good will come out of it.

God says, "I still love Israel, and I will one day raise her up among the nations, but now she is a young child. I must teach her good manners, and I must discipline her as any good parent would."

CLOSED BORDERS

Over-sensitive and offended as a nation, Israel will close her borders to all foreign travel a number of times. Feeling picked on but citing national security as the reason for this action, Israel will overreact and cause nations to resent her arrogant stance. Even some of her most trusted allies will become nervous over her immature reactionary posture.

Israel, however, will learn quickly as a nation and will realign herself with the global community.

God will faithfully fulfill all He has spoken concerning this special nation among the nations. The 21st century will witness Israel coming into her finest hour, but only after some very trying times politically, economically, and spiritually.

ITALY

God's Discipline

Although God deeply loves Italy, she will be racked by natural disasters and a paralyzed economy. She will reap what she has sown, the result of her pride and independence.

In almost every area she will experience difficulty. God will allow these events to occur. He will eventually use these humbling experiences to draw Italy to Himself, although for a season she will resent God.

HUMBLED BY DISASTER

Rome will be humbled and experience her largest and deadliest earthquake ever.

Northern Italy will experience disastrous weather that will cripple her regional economy.

Central and southern Italy will experience high unemployment.

Italian exports will drop to a new low.

Still, the purposes of God will one day be fulfilled for this beautiful nation. She will play a key role in God's plan for the Mediterranean basin, especially in the evangelizing of **Africa**.

JAPAN

Repentance and Revival

G od says, "Japan has much to learn, but I am a great teacher, and she will be a great student. She will learn well that I am the one and only true God."

GOD'S HEAVY HAND

God's hand of judgment will come down heavily on Japan, and her economy will stagnate. God will bring Japan to her knees once again — the result of an economic war between her and God.

God will capture the heart of the Japanese people through a series of events on a national scale that will cause national repentance. These events will be economic, political, and meteorological in nature.

NATIONAL REVIVAL

This wave of national repentance will prepare Japan for a great national revival — one unprecedented in her history.

As a result of this great revival, Christian literature will pour out from Japan's new Christian authors and will impact the nations.

Mega churches will flourish, several of which will have memberships of six to seven thousand.

THE MIDDLE EAST

Trouble's Brewing

The Middle East will once again erupt into a terrible war, the worst yet.

God's mercy, however, will once again supernaturally defend Israel during this non-nuclear event. Although the threat of a nuclear exchange will exist, it will not manifest. God will not allow it.

Much confusion will reign, however, as the devil attempts to destroy Israel again. Former enemies will become allies, and former allies will become enemies. Consequently, a new confederacy of evil will rise up to take off the head of Israel, but it will be short lived and will fail miserably.

Thousands of lives will be sacrificed by evil men trying to destroy Israel. Even though her borders will be compromised by invading armies, she will come into her finest hour and ultimately win a great victory.

DANCING IN THE STREETS

Jerusalem, the holy city of God, will know that God dwells within her walls once again. She will shine with the radiance of her God.

There will be dancing in the streets, and the worldwide Christian Church will be filled with songs about Jerusalem's great triumph over darkness.

NEW ZEALAND

God's Favor

The Church in New Zealand will wonderfully overflow her borders, touching the world with her unique brand of revival fire.

What God does there for the next ten to fifteen years will only be preparatory for something far greater.

Even the physical ground will bubble up with excitement — a sign from God of His approval to this nation.

PEOPLE WILL COME

Internally, the Church will grow at a rate too great for its leaders to handle. This growth spurt will be a good thing, not a bad thing!

Consequently, God will send ministers to places all over the world from this tiny island nation.

People will come from all over the world to New Zealand to be empowered! The country's airports will not be able to handle all the traffic as huge conferences draw thousands.

The Church in New Zealand will take on an international appearance, diverse in its ethnicity and forever changed by the sovereign hand of God. Internationally attended training centers will open, teaching on miracles and healing.

Unusual miracles will be recorded on video during special healing rallies held in the capital city.

Asians will flock there to experience the raw power of God.

God says to New Zealand, "Do not underestimate your role in the new millennium. I will use you as never before in your history."

NORTH & SOUTH KOREA

Two Shall Become One

As the threat of a nuclear exchange lingers over the land, North and South Korea will unite quickly and quietly — almost in a single day!

It will be a marriage made in heaven!

UNITED KOREA

Christianity will flourish as an unexplainable calm settles over this war-torn region.

Western prophets will play an important role in laying the foundations of this new unified Korean Church.

Western aid will come from both secular governments and from the universal church.

The curse of communism will be lifted off the land. As a result, crop production will soar, providing Korea with some of the highest farming yields in all of Asia.

Much pressure will be applied to this United Korea to keep her isolated from the West. **China** will constantly harass this new republic.

Eventually, God will cause the Korean Church to be a mighty influence to the Church in Japan.

PORTUGAL
Tears of Joy

Portugal will weep. At first she will weep for sorrow, then she will weep for joy.

Portugal will weep for God and be known as a nation of mighty intercessors.

NO LONGER IN THE SHADOW

As a nation she will be forgotten no longer. More and more she will be seen on news broadcasts as her role among the nations increases.

Unusual events within her borders will make international news, drawing the attention of the world to her and giving her a new international profile.

Other nations that once despised her will honor her, and nations that ignored her will come to terms with her. Portugal will no longer live in the shadow of other nations.

HUMILITY BEFORE HONOR

A new national humility will blanket Portugal. Thus, her people will hunger for the things of God in unprecedented numbers. Passivity, indifference, and lethargy will disappear, and a new fervor for God will replace centuries of religious performance and pride.

Sudden changes in both her spiritual climate and physical climate will occur. Weather patterns will change, insects will attack, erosion will damage land, frost will hurt harvests, exports will decrease, and imports will increase.

For a time her economy will reel under the hand of God, but all for a good reason.

Portugal will fall to her knees and cry out to God. As a result of this humble plea, God will bless her by reviving her economy and, most importantly, reviving her people unto Him!

God says to Portugal, "Revival is on its way — expect it!"

SAUDI ARABIA
Surprised by God!

The Holy Spirit will also target Saudi Arabia for a great move of God. Thousands will be sovereignly baptized with the Holy Spirit and speak in tongues. Newly converted Arab men will wake up in their beds speaking in tongues and will not even know what they are experiencing.

A new underground church will spring up so quickly that western church leaders will be amazed. Saudi nationals, Christians who have been praying for this very thing, will be sovereignly appointed to lead.

A NEW AND POWERFUL CHURCH

So vast will be this revival that the government of Saudi Arabia will be forced to embrace it instead of fight it.

The nation will experience great internal change as the Holy Spirit sweeps over a spiritually hungry and thirsty population. This turmoil will cause some Christians to quickly leave the country. Many more will stay, thus forming the foundation of this new and powerful Church.

Members of the royal family sympathetic to Christianity will show favor to this fledgling Church, granting it protection against persecution and retaliation of any kind.

Christians around the world will join their Saudi brothers and sisters in singing the old Christian hymn, "To God Be the Glory." Indeed, great things He has done!

NEW WEALTH

In addition to her vast oil reserves, new undiscovered mineral deposits will only add to Saudi Arabia's national wealth.

Eventually, this Arab nation will help finance the spread of the gospel in that region of the world.

SOUTH AFRICA

Pride Comes Before a Fall

South Africa's economy will suffer greatly, yet the Church of South Africa will thrive. There will be difficult times for the nation, but the Church will be filled with many millionaires!

KEPT IN CHECK

Although South Africa's national borders will expand, this nation will be silent for a season as she enters a kind of national hibernation. She will attempt to voice her opinion many times, but her role in international politics will diminish greatly.

South Africa will make attempts and actually cause trouble between nations, especially between **Israel** and the **United States,** but God will keep her in check.

A spirit of confusion, the result of poor national leadership, will rock her political structure to the core.

Her much prized currency will suffer greatly, and foreign investment will decrease. Huge buildings will be purchased for pennies on the dollar, and land will devalue.

ALLIED WITH THE UNITED STATES

Still, the **United States** will strengthen its relationship with South Africa. There will be a strong military alliance between these two nations.

South Africa's mineral wealth will be her biggest national asset, and her need for a strong military presence will be her greatest liability.

A strange new plague will ravage the livestock of South Africa, and food prices will soar.

Food aid from the **United States** will play an important role and will fend off any permanent economic effects.

SOUTH AMERICA
Promotion from the Lord

S outh America will enter a divinely appointed period of rest for the first decade of the new millennium. The Lord will use this critical time to strengthen the Church and establish her as a formidable spiritual force, an army to be reckoned with and even feared.

This wonderful decade-long Sabbath rest will be followed by a sudden awakening, and the continent will burst forth as the leading source of worldwide evangelists. It will be the greatest single release of evangelists from any one continent in the history of the Church.

A SIGN FROM HEAVEN

God will give this continent an unusual sign from heaven to signify this release of worldwide evangelists. Specifically, when islands off her coast begin to crumble and fall into the sea, the great release of South America's evangelists will commence.

This shaking of physical ground will signify the shaking of the heavens over South America and the beginning of major supernatural phenomenon for this region.

Earthquakes will occur where they have never occurred before, and mountains will erupt that have been dormant for centuries. These events will provide further evidence of this continental spiritual awakening. It will be marvelous to behold!

CALLING DOWN FIRE!

These simultaneous events — the worldwide release of evangelists and the domestic release of supernatural signs and wonders — will forever change South America's role in the universal Christian Church.

An Elijah-like anointing will come upon the prophets of South America, and they will actually call down God's fire on all forms of idolatry. These literal displays of power will serve to validate their message, and conversions by the thousands will take place.

In addition, a new order of Bible teacher will also arise, and many books will pour out from South America, stirring the Church to higher heights and deeper depths of commitment to God.

WEATHER CHANGES

South America will experience unprecedented temperature swings in its climate, and weather patterns will literally reverse themselves. Hot will become cold, and cold will become colder — quite the opposite of global warming.

Normal seasonal changes will be unpredictable. All this will cause the ungodly to fear, and the Godly to rejoice. There will be no doubt that Almighty God is visiting this region of the world.

United States of America
Hypocrisy Exposed

In the United States of America there will be great domestic instability during the first ten years of the new century. It will be a time of conservative politics and conservative investment strategies, but the Christian Church will explode with power and authority.

During this same decade, the presidency will change hands several times as the highest office in the land experiences the judgments of God.

Prophets will personally visit the White House, and sincere prayers of repentance will be heard coming from her rooms. A first lady will experience the baptism in the Holy Spirit and receive the gift of speaking in tongues!

CITIES AND STATES

Chicago, Illinois will be host to a prolonged revival. The effects of this revival will last 50 years!

Orlando, Florida will be home to some fantastic miracles! The name Orlando will not only be synonymous with amusement parks, but with miracles — fantastic healings!

Several cities in **Nebraska** will experience an awesome move of God!

As a state, **Nebraska** has been a breadbasket to the nation, providing a tremendous harvest in grain. In dramatic fashion, God will move upon this mid-western state, making it a rich spiritual field, a high yield area for the kingdom of God. Nebraska's rich spiritual soil will feed many who are hungry for more of God.

Also, major foreign investment in this region will raise the standard of living to its highest point ever.

EPILOGUE

PROPHECY IS CONDITIONAL

*Prophecy demands a proper response
to facilitate its fulfillment.*

Most forms of personal predictive prophecy are conditional to some degree and depend on the proper response of the recipient for their accurate and timely fulfillment.

This rule was clearly illustrated in the example of personal prophecy spoken to Bible characters such as King Saul, Gideon, Naaman, and even the nation of Israel. If the conditions were met, the prophecy camepass.

Even today, personal prophecy — whether spoken to individuals or nations — demand a proper response to facilitate its fulfillment. The opposite is equally true, however, since an improper response can disallow it.

Certainly, the prophecies listed in this book will follow the same rule. The final outcome will depend on the proper individual response by the respective continents, regions, nations, states, cities, or individuals.

THE GOD OF THE SECOND CHANCE

What about predictive prophecy that forecasts specific judgments or punishments against a nation? Does God ever rescind such prophetic judgments? Can heartfelt national repentance affect the sentence imposed against a nation by God — thus allowing a nation to avoid His terrible wrath?

As in the example of Jonah and the city of Nineveh, the Bible teaches that a nation can escape God's judgment — even judgments spoken against that nation through prophecy.

First, the God of the Bible is the God of the second chance. With Him there is always hope, even for prodigal nations who have walked away from God.

The nation of Israel proved this point time and time again. Historically, the Israelites would sin, and God would severely judge them through the prophets. Other times, they would repent on a national level, and the prophetic judgment would be abbreviated or avoided altogether. This rule will be equally true in the 21st century.

God is love. He has not changed, and He will continue to show mercy to any nation willing to humble itself and return to Him — but it is their choice. Clearly, the destiny of many nations hangs in the balance.

God does not want to punish these nations. His desire is to bless the nations as any good father would want to bless His children.

Every nation, however, must acknowledge and honor God. No nation can take Almighty God for granted.

There still exists a point of no return, and God help those bastard nations who challenge Him.

IT'S ALL IN THE RESPONSE

Another example of avoiding a prophetic judgment is found in the story of Hezekiah.

The prophet of God told Hezekiah to "get his house in order" because Hezekiah was about to die. Yet God sovereignly decided to spare His life because of Hezekiah's response. God responded out of love and compassion, even altering His initial decision to end Hezekiah's life before His time.

The proper response to a personal prophecy can attract God's best blessing or repel His worse judgment — it's all in the response.

Gideon, Naaman, Hezekiah, and others responded properly and experienced great blessings — even the removal of judgments spoken against them by God.

Others, like King Saul and the children of Israel, responded improperly and experienced all the judgments spoken against them through the prophets. It all depended upon how the individual or nation responded.

Second, prophecy seems to be more of an invitation than anything else.

Prophecy invites us to participate in the will of God. It woos us, lures us, and requests that we respond to it.

Like any invitation, you must respond to it properly in order to benefit from it.

Respond positively, and you reap the benefits. Respond negatively, and you suffer the consequences.

The proper response releases the intrinsic power of that prophecy, causing it to come to pass whether personally or on a national level!

PROPHECY IS LIMITED

Third, prophecy of this kind is never encyclopedic or all inclusive. Rather, predictive prophecy is frequently incomplete. It has definable limits or boundaries.

The Bible teaches, "We know in part and we prophesy in part." Even the most accurate prophecy is limited.

This book — a mere glimpse of a much larger end-times picture — certainly fits that profile. It is an incomplete prophetic message and not meant to be taken as the entire word of the Lord by any means. It is only part of a much greater prophetic picture being painted by the worldwide prophets. I have no doubt that many other prophetic books like this one will follow.

Prophecy is a limited gift with a limited application and should never be viewed as the complete counsel of God in any situation. Many times details are lacking, often purposely omitted by God even in the most accurate of prophecies. Usually, it is just an out-line, a brief overview, a general survey.

Since predictive prophecy is partial, it is not the whole truth. It is simply a part of the truth — God's truth — and should be viewed as such. God is a perfect God, but prophecy is an imperfect gift because imperfect mankind is involved.

PROPHECY SPEAKS TO POTENTIAL

Fourth, prophecy is all about potential.
It speaks to what can be. Often God looks ahead, proclaiming through prophecy His will for a nation — the end result or the "bottom line" from His eternal viewpoint.

There are no guarantees, however, for any nation.

Please pray that God will grant mercy and forgiveness to all nations. Pray that all the good He has planned for them will be experienced — their full potential realized, and their destiny in God secured.

Pray that all the pain and suffering brought upon nations through their own rebellion to God may somehow be avoided.

Remember, nations are about people, and God desperately loves all people.

INDEX

U.S. STATES

CITIES

REGIONS OF THE WORLD

It is an historical fact first century Christians openly embraced and actively participated in the gift of prophecy. They were a very active prophetic laity.

These were not just a few, strange, unapproachable, mystical "prophetic types" sitting on mountaintops somewhere dressed in camel's hair, eating locust and honey, and hearing audible voices. Rather, the entire church body, every man and woman who named the name of Christ understood and experienced the gift of prophecy. They were a prophetic people.

A similar prophetic movement among today's laity is precisely what God is once again restoring to the Church. He is developing a practical yet powerful Church in these last days — again, a prophetic people. He is raising up a prophetic army, a prophetic nation to operate in powerful prophetic giftings. The original prophetic purpose and plan of God for the Body of Christ is coming to pass in our generation!

Follow the way of love and eagerly desire spiritual gifts, especially the gift of prophecy
(I Corinthians 14:1)

Is everything you do a struggle? Does a dark cloud seem to hang over your life?

Are you trapped by feelings of abandonment and betrayal? Does severe hopelessness and chronic loneliness keep you paralyzed in debilitating despair? Are you immobilized by self-doubt and a persistent sense of overwhelming inferiority?

You may be cursed! And you are not alone.

In this startling exposé, Dennis Cramer details his 13-year battle with a "christian" curse and how God not only miraculously exposed the source of the curse, but dramatically delivered him from its devastating effects.

Could you be the victim of spiritual abuse? Could other Christians have pronounced failure and defeat over your life?

In order to bring to light this terrible darkness, Dennis takes you on a journey into the evil world of "christian" witchcraft, "christian" cannibalism, and "christian" curses—where you will not only be informed, but set free!

> *When I read Breaking Christian Curses, my first thought was that every church should have this information.*
> from the foreword by Francis Frangipane, author of The Three Battlegrounds

TO ORDER

You Can All Prophesy
Stepping Out with Integrity
or
Breaking Christian Curses
Finding Freedom from Destructive Prayers
by
Dennis Cramer

Visit
www.arrowbookstore.com

Write to
Arrow Publications
P.O. Box 10102
Cedar Rapids, Ia. 52410

Call
1-319-395-7833
or
Toll Free 1-877-363-6889 (U.S.only)
Fax 1-319-395-7353
VISA/MC/American Express/Discover —Call for shipping costs.